A Walk
in Search
of Meaning

A Walk in Search of Meaning

Discovering God's Pathway through Nature

Dick Watkins

Serenity Mountain Press
Frankfort, Kentucky

A WALK IN SEARCH OF MEANING
Copyright © 2007 by Richard B. Watkins (Dick Watkins)

All rights reserved. No part of this book may be reproduced in any form or by any means, electronic or mechanical, including photocopying, recording, or by any information storage and retrieval system, without prior permission in writing from the author and publisher.

Four lines of a poem appearing on page 65 are from "Why I Fish" Copyright © 2001 by Jimmy D. Moore. Used by permission.

Front and back cover photographs are by the author. The front cover photograph was taken in Breaks Interstate Park in southwest Virginia. The bloodroot wildflowers on the back cover were photographed in early April in Kentucky.

Cover Design: Ginger Watkins

ISBN-10: 0-9770425-0-2
ISBN-13: 978-0-9770425-0-0

Library of Congress Card Number: 2006901965

Serenity Mountain Press
1 Warwick Lane
Frankfort, KY 40601

Printed in the United States of America on acid-free paper containing 30% recycled fiber.

CONTENTS

                                                  Page

- **Preface**   7

- **Acknowledgments**   9

- **Discovering Wildflowers**   11
  - Wildflowers and Us   12
  - Oh Trillium   15
  - Rejoice in the Wildflowers   17
  - Rhododendron Blooming   20
  - Big Eddy Sabbath   22
  - Compassionate God   24

- **Hiking and Backpacking**   31
  - Hiking to Eternity   32
  - Lost on Raven Fork   41
  - Roan Mountain Joy   44
  - Deep Creek Trail in Early Spring   49
  - Mount Rogers Highlands   54
  - North Georgia Uniqueness   58
  - White Blaze Marks and Our Spiritual Journey   61

CONTENTS

    Page

- **Trout Fishing** — **65**
  - Trout Fisherman's Soul — 66
  - Fishing for Trout and People — 69
  - Fishing Smoky Mountain Gems with a Good Friend — 73
  - Big Snowbird Brookies — 81

- **Reflecting** — **87**
  - Appalachian Friendship — 88
  - Backyards, A Life's Journey — 91
  - Simple or Complex? — 101
  - Humankind and Nature: Friend and Foe — 105

- **Praying** — **109**
  - A Prayer for Discernment — 110
  - Pink Lady Slipper Prayer — 112

- **Biographical Sketch** — **115**

PREFACE

There are two major reasons why I have written this collection of memoirs and essays. First, I was challenged by a book by Julie Salamon entitled "Rambam's Ladder: A Meditation on Generosity and Why It Is Necessary to Give."[1] Rambam is an acronym for Rabbi Moses ben Maimon, who lived during the twelfth century. He envisioned a hierarchy of giving to others or a "ladder of charity" with eight rungs going from lowest to highest.

"Rambam's Ladder" describes the first rung of the ladder as giving to others begrudgingly. I'll skip the second through sixth rungs for brevity. The seventh rung represents giving anonymously to someone you don't know, and the eighth or top rung represents giving someone self-reliance. This suggests that the most satisfaction to the giver comes from mentoring others. The saying, "Give them a fish and they will eat for a day, but teach them how to fish and they will eat for a lifetime," also describes Rambam's top rung.

Throughout my business career as a technical manager, I found that mentoring gave me the most long-term satisfaction. Writing about some of my growing experiences and perspectives seemed to be a way of giving or mentoring others while gaining satisfaction for myself.

The second reason for writing this collection of memoirs and essays is that for over thirty-seven years I have had a passion for observing and learning about God's world of nature. Nature always seemed to provide me with excitement and serenity. These contrasting emotions regenerate the spirit. Many times while in nature, I could feel God's overwhelming presence. The feeling of being connected to God and seeing the beauty and order that the Creator has provided, has always given me comfort in the knowledge of God's active participation in the ever-changing universe.

I never seemed to have enough time to explore these passions because of work and child-rearing responsibilities. But reflecting back on these visits to the forests, balds, and streams of the southern Appalachian Mountains with friends and family has had a profound impact on my view of the world and life itself. Similar experiences of the closeness of God have occurred for me in local parks and across the country in many diverse natural environments.

I have been a Christian since my youth, but my main spiritual growth has been in more recent years. The observations, experiences, and perspectives that I describe have helped me grow in body, mind, and spirit. Because of the continuing need for spiritual growth, I conclude the book with prayers for discernment and of comfort. God's spiritual map has many pathways besides nature and prayer. All experiences of life are opportunities to seek and serve God in different ways. It is my hope that these pages will encourage the reader to discover the best way to feel God's presence, to use those opportunities to grow spiritually, and to demonstrate compassion to others.

[1] Rambam's Ladder, Workman Publishing, New York, 2003

ACKNOWLEDGMENTS

I want to thank those who contributed to making this collection of memoirs and essays possible. It starts with two individuals who passed their love of nature on to me when a new job took us to Asheville, NC, after completing our formal education.

Dr. Charles Lindsley (deceased) took my wife and me on an early April morning hike in 1968 to observe wildflowers in bloom. It was our first time to enjoy these little beauties. It was also a life broadening experience for which I will always be grateful. Similarly, Mr. Pat Price introduced me to backpacking in the spring of 1969, and mentored me along the trail, thus enhancing my love of nature and opening up a new, profound way to connect with God. I am grateful to Pat for his friendship over the years, and for his introducing me to this new pathway to God, and for the resultant serenity and excitement.

I am thankful to my wife, Nancy, for her spiritual leadership and guidance over our forty-four years of marriage, and her ideas and critiques that contributed immensely to this collection. Mr. Nick Petit, who was the first to read most of the collection, made many suggestions for improvement in a gentle way that encouraged me, a first-time author. Nancy and Nick also proofread the entire text and made additional editing suggestions.

Rev. John Hunt volunteered many hours to edit this manuscript and mentored me during the process. I am indebted to him for sharing his knowledge and wisdom with me.

I acknowledge the help of Ms. Ginger Watkins for the cover design and file conversions. The staff at McNaughton and Gunn, Inc., Saline, Michigan, was very professional and helpful in the process of their printing of the book.

Most important to acknowledge are the many friends and family members who shared these experiences with me over more than thirty-seven years, and helped me to grow in my relationship with God and to have a better understanding of nature.

DISCOVERING WILDFLOWERS

How many Flowers fail in Wood--
Or perish from the Hill--
Without the privilege to know
That they are Beautiful--

How many cast a nameless Pod
Upon the nearest Breeze--
Unconscious of the Scarlet Freight--
It bear to Other Eyes--

Emily Dickinson

Wildflowers and Us

Wildflowers inspire my passion for intricate beauty and diversity. Their unheralded appearance illustrates the harmony God intended in all of creation. Unless someone has passed on to us the joy of their discovery most of us don't see these tiny treasures. We are all too aware of the hoards that spring up unwanted in our well-tended lawns.

Many delicate species are to be found in old growth forests in early spring before the leaves cast their shadows. In the spring of 1968 a friend and colleague took my wife and me to the Bat Cave, North Carolina, area to introduce us to wildflowers. His passion for wildflowers was quickly passed on like a skilled professor's subject is transmitted to students. My observation skills grew as I searched for wildflowers under the tall trees on a carpet of last year's fallen leaves and needles.

In early spring the bloodroot bursts through the forest floor with its one round, hand-shaped leaf and one snow-white flower. It is arrayed with eight to twelve long, narrow petals and a yellow center, its stem lacing through a deep slit in the leaf palm. Its fragile and enchanting beauty announces the arrival of spring. Usually bloodroot are scattered in small groupings throughout the forest. Viewing a hillside of bloodroot in bloom is a rare and euphoric experience. One such place is Cove Spring Park in Frankfort, Kentucky. Since the blossoms last only a few days, viewing must be well timed. Seeing these blossoms underscores the truth that life is fleeting, and new beginnings are part of the life cycle.

Some wildflowers are resilient, flourishing anywhere, while others can survive only in specific soil and climate conditions. The violet for example can live almost anywhere while the pink lady slipper requires a specific fungus in the soil to survive. Species of wildflowers are as endless as they are diverse. Some types seem to be loners growing by themselves. Others obviously love community with other species. As they force their way up through the dead leaves and needles from years past, they seem to possess willpower, their delicate form belying their strength.

The contemplative soul in us may take a lesson from the wildflowers. Qualities found among these quiet beauties can inspire our highest and best outlook and forbearance. The human species is diverse in personality, from those who barely survive amid great wealth and comfort to the hardy and joyous soul that is optimistic in spite of great pain and hardship.

Symbolism from wildflower forms can relate the cultures of the world to their religions. Dogwood flowers with their four petals remind us of the cross of Jesus Christ. The seven-petal starflower symbolizes the Jewish Menorah with its seven candles as a light to all nations. The spring beauty, with its five white petals streaked with pink, recalls the Five Pillars of Islam and prayer to Allah five times a day. Perennial flowers have annual death and rebirth to a new incarnation reminiscent of the Hindu faith.

Wildflowers reflect a harmonious design for life on Earth. They are a part of creation that speaks of peace, beauty, and serenity. Sight of a group of the delicate and tiny four-petaled bluets, perched on a mossy rock next to a gurgling brook, speaks to that truth. So does the splendor of a small colony of yellow lady slippers blooming in a secluded area. The flower has a central yellow pouch that looks like a moccasin and two lateral petals that resemble twisted ribbons. Take as an example of harmony, the trillium, fire pink, foamflower, Solomon's seal, and Virginia bluebells all living in the same neighborhood.

Their example behooves us to realize nature is telling us that we belong to one big diverse family. We would do well to take a lesson from the wildflowers and learn to live together in harmony. Each variety of the human family adds beauty and meaning to the whole. The peace and meaning we all crave is available to all who will learn from the humble wildflowers.

Oh Trillium

To botanists, trillium wildflowers are classified as monocotyledons in a genus of the lily family. These technical words don't capture the essence of the trillium. I am thrilled by their beauty, intrigued by their diversity, and admire their similarities as well. The trillium's three leaves, whether large or small, exhibit similarities of brothers and sisters or parent and child, however, their flowers, all with three petals show as much diversity as we find among ourselves.

Some trillium flowers are easily seen standing erect above the leaves. They come in a variety of colors: dark red, maroon-purple, pink, yellow, and white. My favorite is the painted trillium, which has snow-white petals with purple V's painted at the base of each of the three petals. These form a large purple triangle as viewed from above. Some hide their beauty beneath their leaves out of sight of the casual observer. These appropriately named nodding trilliums come in a variety of colors: maroon-purple, pink and white. Largest of the trillium flowers is the Vasey's nodding trillium, which has dark maroon-purple flowers. Its flowers can be easily overlooked, since they are hidden below its very large leaves. Missed opportunities in our lives are experiences that we all share. Perhaps the close attention required in finding the tiny wildflowers on the forest floor could teach us how to discover new opportunities around us.

As I hike through the mountains and valleys it is wonderful to find a hillside community of large-flowered trillium with their very large white petals, and then further along to find a community of yellow sessile trillium with their long and narrow yellow petals. This segregation comes about due to the difficulty of distant propagation of seeds, and safety of the local environment.

As a youth I grew up in an all-white town in Kentucky; it was safe, and enjoyable, but I didn't experience diversity. Only when I had a summer job in a large city did I first experience being a minority. At first it frightened me, but later, gave me a new perspective. I vividly remember my walk along the "Stations of the Cross"[1] in Jerusalem, following Jesus' path to His death on the cross, walking the path with fellow Christians of all colors and ethnicities. It was a joyous experience of commonality and diversity, so like the trillium family of wildflowers.

[1]Also called "Way of the Cross" or "Via Dolorosa" in Latin

Rejoice in the Wildflowers

The rainforests of South America and South Asia may have the greatest variety of plant species anywhere on Earth, but I delight in the myriad of spring wildflowers that bloom much closer to home, in the southern Appalachian Mountains. My wife and I go wildflower hiking with a group of friends from Kentucky in April. We can usually identify about fifty different species of spring wildflowers in bloom during two or three days on the trail. Poplar Cove Loop Trail in Joyce Kilmer Memorial Forest with its one-hundred-foot tall tulip popular and hemlock trees is my favorite. Two of my favorite wildflowers, the painted trillium and the showy orchis, are in bloom at that time. These hikes reveal a diverse community of plants living in ecological harmony in this virgin forest. No kudzu spoils the scenery. The tulip poplars are not yet leafed out so there is plenty of light on the forest floor. By May the poplar leaves cast their shadows, and the forest has a completely different atmosphere. Then it has the feel of hiking in a dark, humid, canopied rainforest.

    The effect of elevation on the blooming season for wildflowers is notable. The bloodroot may be in full bloom at 1500 feet elevation, while up the same trail at 2500 feet elevation it may not even be out of the ground. If it is barely out of the ground, it requires keen observation to see its new flower and leaf stems forcing their way through last season's fallen leaves. At this stage there is a tightly coiled leaf wrapped around two stems. The young plant looks like a one to two inch long green stick coming out of the ground. It is fascinating to see the stages of growth of the bloodroot with one stem growing taller with a white flower bud on top, followed by the unfurling of the green leaf atop the second stem, and finally the opening of the beautiful flower with its white petals and yellow center. To see the bloodroot in full bloom at 2500 feet elevation requires traveling several hundred miles farther south. After its flower dies the hand-like leaf continues to grow to as much as eight inches in diameter.

On any wildflower trail some species live in large, segregated groups; others are found in a potpourri of many different species living together; and still others appear recluse-like. Those that appear solitary nonetheless have special adaptations to allow them to survive under specific conditions. There is a mysterious bliss that overtakes me upon discovering several jack-in-the-pulpits or yellow lady slippers in bloom. I proudly announce my discovery to others in the group and share my enthusiasm. Farther down the trail there are colonies of wild geranium, dwarf iris, purple phacelia, and blue phlox. Sharing these small, unexpected packages of God-made beauty with others inspires me.

Wildflowers wait unassumingly in the dense forest away from the noise and bustle of our society. Although their habitat is receding due to human construction, they do not cry out in protest. The buildings that humans construct are often our badges of success, efficiency, or comfort, demanding to be noticed. Small wonder that the contemplative soul yearns for the serenity and quiet of the spaces inhabited by the modest species of divine creation.

Wherever humans live in close proximity it is essential for them to be flexible and tolerant. Those who cannot adapt to living with others may find themselves isolated by their own intolerance. Drawing a lesson from wildflowers we can be inspired to seek harmony in diversity. The divine design of the bloodroot affords a simple example for us. The give and take required for living in community is a small price to pay for the dividends of shared experiences and meaning. From a tiny narrow view of human society when we are babies and children we stretch, grow, and unfurl to reach out to others in our loving and caring. Those who do this well will thrive.

Life's daily joys usually come in small, unexpected packages, such as the time a stranger offers assistance with a car that won't start, or when a longtime friend that now lives faraway sends a letter or an e-mail just to keep in touch. Life in our busy, complex society is enriched by daily sharing small gifts of care with others. Wildflowers of the forest enrich our lives when we contemplate their simplicity and adaptability.

Rhododendron Blooming

I go hiking in the southern Appalachian Mountains in the summer to see the rhododendron blooming. Walking along the ridge-tops in late June one comes upon grassy bald areas with large islands of catawba rhododendron: magnificent broadleaf, evergreen shrubs dressed in lavender and purple flowers. These remind me of the formal gardens of Versailles and Chenonceaux, but this is God's garden. It's also a superb lunch stop.

For the short distance walker, two of our countries largest displays of catawba rhododendron can be seen at Craggy Gardens and Roan Mountain, North Carolina. Another large garden is at Rhododendron Gap, Virginia. But I like best the unexpected gardens that I come upon when hiking the Appalachian Trail (AT). They are calm and serene places inviting one to meditate.

In July, hiking down a trail from the ridge-top towards the valley, I anticipate seeing the wonderful rosebay rhododendron. They can grow twenty feet tall. When viewed from above, they look like a forest embedded in a canopy of hemlock and tulip poplar. The flowers are white globular clusters composed of many funnel-shaped blossoms. A mountainside in bloom can move me to ecstasy!

Rosebay rhododendron thickets are almost impossible to walk through, but the deer love to bed-down in them for safety. Fortunately for us, trail-makers have cut paths through and under the tangled branches to make marvelous tunnels for us to enjoy the rosebay from a different perspective.

As a trout fly fisherman I consider the rosebay rhododendron a nuisance as well as a blessing. It is a struggle to weave in and out among their branches and large leaves to get to a trout stream lined with the rosebay rhododendron. Their dark green leaves hanging over the stream are beautiful, but are likely to snare an imperfectly cast dry fly. These leaves, the thickest and toughest in the southern Appalachian Mountain forest, are a real challenge to the trout fisherman. The joy of being in God's garden overcomes the frustration of repeated attempts to rescue the dry fly.

Rosebay rhododendron leaves even indicate the air temperature. The long, narrow leaves droop and curl longitudinally to prevent the loss of leaf moisture as the temperature falls below freezing. This built-in protection is a marvelous illustration of the providence of nature.

The human spirit needs renewal from the stress and rush of our culture. Walking among the protected and secret spaces beneath these marvelous bushes affords a new perspective to life. There is serenity here that money can't buy nor fame provide. Nature is witness to divine generosity and care for all creatures.

The serene quiet of the rhododendron thicket affords a realization of blessings from God that often goes unnoticed. If I can have several days each summer to walk among the blooming rhododendron, I will be refreshed for another year.

Big Eddy Sabbath

As a young child my wife lived in a winterized summer camp on the Kentucky River a couple of miles upstream from Frankfort near Big Eddy Beach. The beach she played on and the camp she lived in are still there after sixty years.

Several years ago my friend, Don, showed me several very accessible places near home, where there are many different wildflower varieties. One of those places is a hillside near Big Eddy Beach. On a Sunday morning in mid April, Don told me that the white trout lilies near Big Eddy Beach should be in bloom that day. He had been there four days earlier, and the buds were up, but not blooming yet. Since the flowers live for only a couple of days, after a late lunch I drove right out Big Eddy Road to the appropriate spot. Walking back toward town, I immediately saw many varieties of wild flowers in bloom on the hillside just off the road. They included yellow trout lilies, wood poppies, squirrel corn, dutchman's breeches, spring beauty, cut-leaf toothwort, sessile trillium, false rue anemone, blue phlox, ginger, and Jacob's ladder. All were living together within a fifty-yard segment of the road. They were all breathtaking in the mid-afternoon sun.

Seeing the wildflower diversity it's easier to accept the importance of diversity in all life forms, including our own species. Diversity provides synergism and complexity to our lives to enhance the richness of our communities.

Returning to my excursion near home, I retraced my steps and passed the car and then went around the big curve in Big Eddy Road to behold an immense green and white garden of trout lilies the size of about two basketball courts set side-by-side, but tilted at a forty-five degree angle up the hillside. It was an incredible view from below, but I had to climb the steep hillside to sit among these amazing lilies. Their heads were bowed as if in God's presence. Their leaves were mottled with brown spots, similar to the back of a brook trout, thus the name trout lily. The forty-five minutes or so that I was there people worked in their yards across the road. Others passed by in cars and on bicycles without stopping, missing the beauty. I felt privileged to sit and meditate among these dainty wildflowers. I felt joy, serenity, and the overwhelming presence of God.

Experience enabled me to observe a trout lily leaf pushing up a dead oak leaf. It had suspended the dead leaf in mid-air, piercing the dead oak leaf as it pushed up through last year's leaf-covered ground.

Contemplating the experience in the lily garden, I wonder why I was privileged as to be at this special place just at the right time to enjoy such beauty. What would it be like if all days were as wonderful as that day, when I could talk to good friends and family in the morning and experience the beauty of the white trout lily garden in the afternoon. Would we appreciate these simple joys that I experienced that day so much if we didn't have painful days as well? I can remember years ago when we lived in Asheville, North Carolina, all the longtime residents were going to the beach for their vacation, while my wife and I wanted to enjoy the southern Appalachian Mountains. We couldn't understand why they chose to leave. The every-day routine at home, even with its beauty, moves people to want to see new vistas. Sometimes we miss the best right before us because even beauty can become our "ordinary." The white trout lily garden on the hillside near Big Eddy Beach in mid April each year is one of my special nearby outdoor shrines.

Is there a special place near your home waiting for you to discover it?

Compassionate God

The psalmist cries out, "What are human beings, that you think of them; mere mortals, that you care for them?"[1] The night sky revealed God's handwork and elicited from the psalmist a feeling of awe. Human beings seem to be quite insignificant when contemplating the vastness of space or the number of stars that the eye can see on a clear night. With our powerful telescopes, we can see much more and the question is even more poignant.

What is the evidence that God cares for us? One source is from another psalm, "The Lord is good to everyone and has compassion on all he made."[2] This Bible scripture is a starting point for our exploration.

Majestic old growth forests in the Appalachian Mountains provide havens for contemplation of the Creator's work. Observing wildflowers on the forest floor has given me a feeling of tranquility far exceeding the time I have spent in these forests. Feeling God's presence during these wildflower sojourns has shaped my life, and has led me to know that He cares for us.

We demonstrate how wildflowers inspire us by using them to represent our states. North Carolina, Virginia, and Alaska chose the jack-in-the-pulpit, the Virginia bluebells, and the forget-me-not, respectively.

The bluet's brilliant four petals in the shape of a Maltese cross startle the discoverer at their quiet beauty. The jack-in-the-pulpit with its upright member is reminiscent of a pastor giving a sermon based on the Holy Scriptures. The bleeding heart with its red heart-shaped blossoms symbolizes love and empathy for others. The wild rose, spreading as it does by underground runners, witnesses to sharing love.

The lavender passion flower is a tendril-climbing vine reminding us of Jesus' instructions, "I am the vine, and you are the branches. Those who remain in me, and I in them, will bear much fruit; for you can do nothing without me." [3]

The hearts-a-bustin' plant vividly suggests having compassion for others. The crimson fruit bursts open in September exposing brilliant red-orange seeds. The juicy fruit and seeds provide food for the birds. Symbolically, the plant could represent Jesus "feeding the five thousand" both nutritionally and spiritually, and encouraging us all to be compassionate to others in need.

Wildflowers are used as symbols in the world's religions. In Buddhism the lotus flower is a symbol of perfect joy and wisdom.

> "The lotus has its roots in the mud,
> Grows up through the deep water,
> And rises to the surface.
> It blooms into perfect beauty and purity in the sunlight.
> It is like the mind unfolding to perfect joy and wisdom" [4]

Hinduism also uses the lotus flower to honor Brahma, God-Creator of the universe. Brahma is portrayed sitting on a golden lotus flower. The lotus is the national flower of India. Islam uses flower and plant symbols in its mosques.

Christians recognize the four-petal dogwood flower as a symbol of Jesus' cross and crown of thorns. The Easter lily reminds us of His resurrection. The bloodroot with its pure white petals could signify Jesus' transfiguration on Mount Hermon together with Moses and Elijah. The white lily is a symbol of Judaism as expressed in the Old Testament book of Hosea. "I will be like the dew to Israel; he will blossom like a lily." [5]

As we have seen certain flowers provide believers of many religious traditions a divine connection. Similarly, in these faith traditions compassion is a virtue rooted in the divine. Compassion is defined in Webster's Dictionary as "a feeling of deep sympathy and sorrow for someone struck by misfortune, accompanied by a desire to alleviate the suffering." The heart's-a-bustin' plant exemplifies a figurative bridge between a wildflower and our acts of compassion.

The Buddha, who lived in the 5th Century B.C., made his life work an act of compassion.[6] As Saint Thiruvalluvar, a Tamil Hindu wrote two thousand years ago, "Find and follow the good path and be ruled by compassion. For if the various ways are examined compassion will prove the means to liberation."[7]

In the Qur'an, Holy Scriptures of Islam, all one hundred and fourteen chapters start with the words "In the Name of God, the Merciful, the Compassionate"[8], reminding the believer of the compassionate nature of God. The Prophet Muhammad said, "Oh people, be compassionate to others so that you may be granted compassion by God."

The Fourteenth Dalai Lama of Tibetan Buddhism spoke of the importance of compassion. "If you want others to be happy, practice compassion. If you want to be happy, practice compassion." He received the Nobel Peace Prize in 1989. Mother Teresa, Roman Catholic founder of the Missionaries of Charity, of Calcutta, India, lived as an example of Christian compassion. Her work with the poorest of the poor (untouchables) led to her recognition as a Noble Peace Prize winner in 1979. Although professing very different faith traditions, both Mother Teresa and the Fourteenth Dalai Lama talked and walked the path of compassion.

Compassion is a constant and pervasive trait that Jesus demonstrated while on Earth. The symbol of the cross reminds us of Jesus' suffering, but the example of compassion is central to His ministry. David, my former pastor, said in a sermon, "Compassion is a stronger word than love." I was moved to reflect on his statement.

Jesus said, "Love your enemies and pray for those that persecute you."[9] This scripture means that we can't select just those we want to love, but are challenged by Him to love everyone. Love is an emotion all humans need to experience both as givers and as receivers. The word compassion contains the element of action to help others. The Son of God came to live in a human body to demonstrate that love and compassion are the fundamental values we are to emulate to establish His kingdom on Earth.

During Jesus' ministry in Palestine the poor and the oppressed composed the vast majority of the population. Jesus was part of the very small middle class, but during His ministry He associated mostly with the lower classes because of His compassion for them.[10] There are many examples of this in stories of Jesus' ministry: He healed the sick, multiplied the loaves and the fishes, and befriended a hated Samaritan woman at the well. He used parables such as the "Good Samaritan"[11] and the "Father of the Prodigal Son"[12] that demonstrated compassion from deep down in the heart.

God has given us a beautiful planet, but we must work to sustain it and keep it beautiful. We are not showing compassion for the ills of this planet by cutting down too much forest, burning too much fossil fuel, covering the Earth with asphalt and concrete, piling up waste, and polluting the Earth with heavy metals from our industries. It is not fair that resources of the underdeveloped countries are being depleted for the gain of the developed nations. Justice and compassion are not being demonstrated. It is not fair that large corporations take advantage of cheap labor and resources in developing countries for their own huge profits. It is not just or compassionate of us that millions die of AIDS or from genocide in Africa while we fret over oil supply or illegal immigrants. The list is long and the solutions complex.

God looks down on us and sees our greed, shortsightedness, and lack of compassion. It was in the life of Jesus that we saw compassion best modeled. It was in His life that we saw how much God cares for humans. We ignore that example at our great peril. Even the wildflowers model peace and beauty. As Jesus said, "Look how the wildflowers grow: they do not work or make clothes for themselves. But I tell you that not even King Solomon with all his wealth had clothes as beautiful as one of these flowers."[13]

We run around trying to keep up with the latest style, fad, or craze. Much of what we buy is designed to become obsolete so that we must buy again. Think of how much our country could help the poorest nations if the energy and production for planned obsolescence could be directed toward them.

How often do we follow Jesus' example of compassion? At Christmas time or when there is a major disaster we demonstrate that we care, but at other times we seem to spend more time and resources combating our enemies rather than on peace and compassion for them. We would do well to take a lesson from the lowly hearts-a-bustin' plant. If one has compassion for others, it must originate within one's heart, and "burst" forth from inside to perform acts of caring. Jesus said, "Love your enemies." With prayer and compassion for our enemies, possibly they can become our friends.

We still marvel at the stars, but we are aghast at the precious few untainted virgin lands we have left. These precious places are shrines that speak to us of the Creator and allow us to meditate on the teachings of the scriptures. Henry David Thoreau said, "I went into the woods to live life deliberately.....I came out of the woods because I had other lives to live." [14] God wants each of us to find ways to serve humankind. The implication in Thoreau's words is that each of us should go into the woods to contemplate our life purpose, discover it, and then come out of the woods to carry out that purpose, which certainly includes showing compassion for others. We have more responsibilities in our lives than to feel serenity and know that God is near us. I believe that compassion is that responsibility.

Compassion is a characteristic that seems to grow in us with practice. After the joy experienced from an initial kind act, we become more sensitive to others' problems, and respond again to needs we see. The experience is the Biblical equivalent of the Apostle Paul's quote of Jesus, "It is more blessed to give than to receive." [15]

The amazing universe speaks of God's glory. Our precious forests invite us to contemplate the meaning of creation. When we consider the grandeur and natural beauty of the universe and our place in it, we must surely realize that God cares. The bloodroot, dogwood, bleeding heart, bluet, jack-in-the-pulpit, passion flower, and the hearts-a-bustin' all are our witnesses. Sending His Son to Earth was the greatest illustration of God's compassion for us. No matter our faith tradition, our challenge is to demonstrate the compassion that Jesus demonstrated. He offers life to those who follow His example. Believing that Jesus suffered and died for us acknowledges our acceptance of His grace. Caring for others demonstrates that our belief has matured into action.

[1] Psalms 8:4 (TEV)
[2] Psalms 145:9 (TEV)

[3] John 15:5 (TEV)
[4] http://online.sfsu.edu/~rone/Buddhism/footsteps.htm.
[5] Hosea 14:5 (NIV)
[6] Van Mater, Kirby, "Buddhism: The Path of Compassion," Sunrise, April/May, 1986
[7] Thiruvalluvar, "Thirukkural: The Book of Wisdom," Verse 242
[8] Arberry, A. J. (translator) "The Koran Interpreted," 1955
[9] Matthew 5:44 (NIV)
[10] Nolan, Albert, "Jesus before Christianity," Orbis Books, New York, 1994
[11] Luke 10:30-37
[12] Luke 15:11-32
[13] Matthew 6:28-29 (TEV)
[14] Thoreau, Henry David, "Walden," Dover Publications, Mineola, New York
[15] Acts 20:35 (NIV)

HIKING AND BACKPACKING

In all things of Nature there is something of the marvelous.

Aristotle

Hiking to Eternity

My first backpacking trip was with a group of friends from Asheville in 1969. It was a thirteen-mile weekend hike on the Appalachian Trail (AT) in North Carolina starting from Stecoah Gap, hiking over Cheoah Bald, and ending at Wesser. Young, enthusiastic and confident, I thought I could do anything. Those thoughts evaporated only 200 yards from the start at Stecoah Gap. By then I was already exhausted. The trail was steep, and it was clear to me that I was not physically fit. Could I make it, I wondered; and what should I have left out of the borrowed backpack? Fortunately, that initial 200 yards was one of the steepest of the whole trip. I soon began to enjoy the hike and to appreciate all the native plants, including the yellow-orange flowers of flame azalea in full bloom. Climbing from 3200 feet elevation at Stecoah Gap to the summit of Cheoah Bald at 5062 feet was quite a milestone for me. We had wonderful views of the surrounding mountains in western North Carolina and the Nantahala Gorge below.

In the Cherokee language Nantahala means land of the midday sun, which suggests how deep and narrow the gorge is. It was only a short distance from the summit to the Sassafras Gap shelter or lean-to where we spent the night. The shelter had three sides enclosed and an open front.

Pat invited me to join the group and served as my encourager and mentor for this first trip. New to me were such basics as getting water from the nearby spring, cooking freeze-dried food over a Primus backpacking stove, and sleeping in my sleeping bag on a wire mesh bed in the lean-to. The trip down to Wesser the next day was a lot tougher than I realized it would be. We descended more than 3000 feet in six miles. I discovered that trail hiking downhill is tough on the knees, and because of the tendency of my feet to slide forward in my boots, my toes blistered. That's when I learned the value of moleskin to either protect against blistering or preventing blisters from getting worse.

This trip was a wonderful new experience. It started me on a path that has led me to oneness with nature. I owe much to Pat as my mentor, and to that small group with whom I shared the trip.

From the overall good experience on my first backpacking trip, I decided to buy a backpack. I asked my brother if he would like to take a backpacking trip in the Smoky Mountain National Park. He had enjoyed backpacking so he eagerly agreed. Our father dropped us off at Newfound Gap for a three-day, thirty-three mile, backpacking trip along the Appalachian Trail to I-40.

This trip revealed how much I had to learn about backpacking. It was an overly ambitious hiking plan for us. Both days we made it to the shelters as planned, but we were completely exhausted. The joy was missed because we had overestimated our capabilities.

The first night we slept at Peck's Corner; the second night at Cosby Knob. In the Smokies the shelters had a chain-link fence on the front with a door to protect the campers from animals. Our ignorance asserted itself again the third morning when we threw our leftover breakfast to two black bears approaching us from below.

Fortunately we made it back into the Cosby Knob shelter, and closed the chain-link fence door before the bears got to us. We were safe! After sniffing around the shelter one bear went to the spring nearby, started drinking water, and then ate my bar of soap! When bubbles and foam started coming out of his mouth, he scampered up the mountainside. We concluded that animals, like humans, must learn from their mistakes.

Our Asheville group tried to make one backpacking trip a year. One such hike was to Gregory Bald in the Smokies to see what is claimed to be the largest flame azalea collection in the world. They were gorgeous! We saw several varieties including one with red blossoms as well as the usual yellow-orange blossom varieties. We stayed at a shelter that was off the AT, and just big enough for the four of us. It is a good thing that it slept four! It was in poor condition, and was torn down a few years later, but for us it was a lot better than carrying a tent.

We also hiked a loop trail in the Smokies from Cades Cove up to Russell Field, along the AT to Spence Field, and back down to Cades Cove. We spent the night in the Russell Field shelter.

During this trip we saw two park rangers on horseback. They carried rifles and were trying to shoot some of the wild boar, which were rooting up the ground in the area. Thirty minutes later we heard several gunshots, and suddenly we saw a group of wild boar running. We watched them until they started coming toward us. We scampered back to the shelter, closing the chain-link fence door behind us! The group of wild boar included about six mature males and females all with tusks, plus several piglets. It was nice to be in a shelter with a chain-link fence on the front instead of camping in a tent that day.

Now most of the wild boar have been removed from the Smokies, so the rebuilt shelters such as Ice Water Spring and Cosby Knob don't have chain-link fences on the front. This requires backpackers to be more responsible for keeping their food out of the reach of the black bears. The rules are simple: tie a rope to the food bag and raise the food up in a nearby tree or use the wire hoists that are provided at some shelters and campsites to lift the food high above so the black bears can't get at the food. Mice also can be nuisances to backpackers. If there are no bears around, the unique, hand-made hanging contraptions used in shelters usually keep your food safe from the mice. Prepare these by tying a sturdy string to the shelter ceiling, and then lace the string through a hole in a metal barrier. For this a large empty tuna fish can, mounted up side down, will do. Then tie a knot in the string so the barrier hangs freely from the ceiling. Then tie another string to the knot on the bottom of the barrier, and hang the food bag from it.

Some mice are acrobats that can get around the barrier. So this contraption doesn't always protect the food supply. Also, hearing the mice run around the shelter at night is also disruptive to some of us. Sleeping in a tent, and hanging our food in a tree is sometimes a better option if we don't mind carrying a tent.

Most of the trips our group took covered about seven miles a day, allowing us to arrive at the shelter in plenty of time to rest before setting everything up for supper, and to talk about the day's experiences. Since there are many AT backpackers in the Smokies, the US Park Service requires an advanced reservation for each shelter bed. That meant we usually shared a shelter with strangers. It was good meeting others that had a love for nature, and wanted to share their backpacking stories.

We occasionally backpacked outside the Smokies, and usually didn't see another person. These trips were on the North Carolina and Tennessee border. They included trips from Sam's Gap to Spivey Gap over Big Bald Mountain, and from Allen Gap to the town of Hot Springs, NC, on the French Broad River. On the former trip I was startled by the deafening thunder of the wings of a ruffed grouse taking off in flight. I was so surprised that I didn't see the bird fly off into the forest. On the latter trip I saw a ruffed grouse walking on the trail in front of us just before it skyrocketed off with the sound and speed of a cannonball. In the southern Appalachians these birds are usually reddish-brown and a little smaller than a chicken.

    Our group made only one winter backpacking trip while I lived in Asheville. We started at the Cataloochee Ranger Station where we were each inspected to ensure that we had sufficient gear for the temperatures and potential snow. After getting our permits to spend the night, we backpacked up Balsam Mountain Trail to Laurel Gap shelter near Big Cataloochee Mountain. There we spent the night. We sounded like a large army as we crunched the leaves on the trail. When we stopped, the complete silence was a startling contrast. In the early evening from our shelter we watched the stars disappear and a shroud of clouds move in. The air temperature dropped below freezing. The next morning to our surprise the sun awakened us to a marvelous sparkling fairyland with sunlight reflecting off of every tree limb and twig! Rime ice coated everything. The sight will be forever etched in my memory.

    Rime ice is common in the southern Appalachian Mountains. It is formed from microscopic water droplets that are super-cooled in clouds that pass around a mountain. The tree limbs and twigs serve as nucleation sites, and the super-cooled water droplets condense immediately, and freeze upon contact with the tree limbs and twigs that are below 32°F to form the beautiful rime ice coating.

    We backpacked along Mount Sterling Ridge Trail to Mount Sterling through trees covered with rime ice, a magnificent sight in the bright sunlight. When we reached Mount Sterling Fire Tower it was too icy to climb the tower for a better view, so we continued on to Mount Sterling Gap where we had left my car. To our complete shock my car was not where I parked it! A frantic search led us to the car, which had been pushed over the hillside out of sight. With a team effort we were able to get it back up onto the gravel road. We felt relief since we were ten miles from our other car, and on a gravel road with very little traffic. Probably some local kids enjoyed doing that trick, but it did not diminish our experience of the magnificent hike.

Pat's mentoring in backpacking taught me enough to mentor others. My wife, Nancy, and I planned to take our four-year-old and eight-year-old daughters for a two-night backpacking trip with everyone carrying their fair share of the weight in their packs. For this first trip we went to the Smokies on Friday after work, backpacked only about one mile from the trailhead up Noland Creek to Bear Pen Branch campsite, and set up the two tents. Our supper was mainly freeze-dried food cooked over a backpacking stove. On Saturday morning we broke camp and backpacked another two miles up Noland Creek to Mill Creek campsite. When we got there the girls enjoyed playing in the stream, and I did a little trout fishing. There wasn't any rain on this trip, which certainly made it more enjoyable as we backpacked the three miles out to our car on Sunday afternoon. There was no contact with another human being on the trip until we were nearly back to our car and met a man that was trout fishing. What a joy to observe that our children, now grown, have the same admiration for God's works of art in nature continuing in their souls today.

When we moved to Kentucky and the girls were older we took backpacking and hiking trips with other families and shared experiences such as watching a bear picking and eating berries from a tall bush. Also, we enjoyed seeing our daughters and others learn to dry fly fish and catch trout. As many know, mentoring someone is a joyful experience for the mentor no matter what the activity.

After our daughters had left home, Nancy and I decided to take a late fall backpacking trip in Kentucky. Randy, a friend from Frankfort, recommended this particular hike as a good two-day hike with good views. It was a weekend getaway in mid November 1994, after the leaves were off the trees. Our plan was to drive to Middlesboro, Kentucky, and Cumberland Gap, leave our car at Pinnacle Overlook on the Kentucky-Virginia border, and do a point-to-point hike from there along Cumberland Mountain's Ridge Trail to Gibson Gap to spend Saturday night. On Sunday we planned to hike down from the top on Gibson Gap Trail to US58 where we would call a taxi to pick us up and take us back to our car at Pinnacle Overlook.

We started out backpacking on Saturday. The day was gorgeous and sunny, but cold, and standing in Kentucky and Virginia we could see views of Cumberland Gap and Tennessee. Since the leaves were off the trees, and the air was so clear, we could see a long way north into Kentucky and imagine the Wilderness Road going through a gap in Pine Mountain in the distance. The Wilderness Road was the major route through which people immigrated to Kentucky and further west. Three hundred thousand people passed through Cumberland Gap on the Wilderness Road by 1800. To the south and east we saw farmland below with mountains beyond. We were told to be sure to take plenty of water with us since there would not likely be any spring at Gibson Gap for us to prepare our meals Saturday evening and Sunday morning. We had dressed for the cold weather and the backpacking was great. It was about five miles to Gibson Gap, and we got there in plenty of time to set up our tent and have supper before it got dark.

We had brought our heavy sleeping bags, and it was a good thing, because the temperature kept dropping throughout the night due to the clear skies. Before we went to bed we could see the lights very clearly in the town of Harrogate, Tennessee, about five miles away, but the silence was deafening. I got up in the middle of the night, and was awestruck at the incredible night sky. The millions of stars of the Milky Way Galaxy made me feel that there is no way a human can envision the immensity of God's universe. I felt insignificant as a mere human in God's presence, but knew that God cares for all of us on planet Earth, and wherever else life exists.

The next morning when we got up it was about 20°F, and we quickly got the backpacking stove out to heat water for hot drinks and cereal. I picked up the plastic water bottle, and to my dismay it was frozen solid! Since the water was in a plastic bottle, it couldn't be heated, and I wasn't sure what to do. Then I remembered that I had left the other plastic bottle in one of the backpacks, and fortunately it was embedded in some clothes, which served as insulation, so we got plenty water out of the bottle for our breakfast. It shows how important little details can be.

After packing we started down Gibson Gap Trail, which was very steep, giving Nancy some blisters on her toes in her too short boots. This trail was not marked very well, but then it turned into a logging road so everything seemed just fine until the logging road ended in a meadow. Where do we go now? Since we got on the logging road at least a mile back, we decided to continue on through the meadow, to see what we could find.

Eventually we got to the top of a little knoll, and were able to see cattle grazing in a fenced field ahead of us, so we decided there must be a farmhouse around there somewhere. As we walked along the fence of the pasture Nancy noticed that the next field seemed to be greener and mowed. Then I noticed several individual upright sticks in the field, and one looked like it had a flag on it; and as you guessed, it was a golf course that we had discovered! As we backpacked along the fairway we finally saw what probably was the clubhouse, and then we saw a couple of golfers. We went to the clubhouse, and said that we were lost, and needed to give directions to a driver to pick us up. As it turned out the driver knew where the golf course was, and it all worked out fine. We had a good backpacking experience, but it was rather embarrassing for seasoned backpackers to get lost. We came out onto US58 about a mile east of where we had intended.

I have learned from experience that when I am summer hiking always to be on the lookout for those special little patches of wild blueberries that have just ripened. These wild blueberries are about one-fifth the size of cultivated blueberries, but have at least twice the flavor. Somehow eating these delicious little morsels is a soul connection to God for me like the Israelites receiving manna from heaven during their wandering in the wilderness. I know not to eat too many of them because the birds will sound off that these morsels are for them and the other animals nearby for sustaining their lives. However, for me eating a small handful of these wild blueberries somehow symbolizes partaking of communion in God's presence.

Due to my back's load carrying limitations caused by osteopenia, I have had to stop backpacking and switch to day hiking. We go with a group of friends from Frankfort to Fontana Village Resort, North Carolina, to participate in the Spring Wildflower Week. The day hiking gives me the same euphoric feeling of exploration of God's world with many wildflowers to see in bloom, and it is special doing it with friends. I am still blessed that I can hike, and maybe a little wiser; but fortunately we don't know God's plan for us, so I seek the joy in my soul that comes from hiking in the southern Appalachians as long as I can.

Lost on Raven Fork

Many years ago, when I was still a relatively new student of hiking in the backcountry, I took a late April backpacking trip with my wildflower mentor. We went to one of the most remote areas of the Smoky Mountain National Park called the Three Forks area of Raven Fork.

The two of us hiked a loop trail on a weekend backpacking trip. We hiked up Hyatt Ridge, a 1000-foot ascent from Round Bottom Campground on Beech Gap Trail until it hit Hyatt Ridge Trail. Then we followed Hyatt Ridge Trail until we came to the campsite at McGee Springs, where we stopped to eat our lunch and fill our water bottles from the spring. This part of the trip was all on regular types of graded and marked trails.

To my surprise, at that point our journey got a lot more difficult. On the way down into the wilderness area a lot of the hike was on what is called a "man-way," which means that it is a trail that is no longer maintained. It probably had had no maintenance for many years, and didn't have trail blazes to mark the way. Many trees had fallen across the trail, and we had to either climb over or go under the trees with our backpacks, sometimes crawling in the mud. That was really exhausting. I thought we were never going to get to our destination: the campsite on the big pool. Three small streams come together to form Raven Fork and the big pool. It was appropriately named Three Forks Pool.

The spot was beautiful and serene with the calm, green-colored pool and with the sound of the gentle flowing water entering the back end of the pool. It was special after the long exhausting hike on the "man-way." We camped right by the large pool in an area that was open compared to the forested areas through which we had hiked all day. I fished for brook trout in the big pool, but, as I recall, didn't catch any even though I got a lot of strikes. One of the highlights of that Saturday was seeing the largest group of large-flowered trillium that I have ever seen. The whole hillside was covered with their blossoms. I felt a sense of awe at the beauty of God's world, and will never forget the experience. I have always wanted to take my family back to that mountainside to share my experience.

On Sunday we started down Raven Fork. Again there was no real trail. Sometimes we would walk in the stream, and other times on a small, faint trail along one or the other bank. None of these trails was marked. Perhaps the difficulty of the trail explained why we had not seen other hikers. I would stop occasionally to fish.

The combination of fishing and backpacking was made more difficult because of the extra gear I carried. I had the backpack, camping gear, hiking boots, the fly rod, fishing supplies, and sneakers for trout fishing.

I remember one spot in particular where a waterfall entered the main stream. It was a contemplative place so I stayed there just admiring the sheer beauty. Also, it was the perfect spot for casting a dry fly for trout, which I did. My mentor did not fish and got impatient with me, and said that he was going to hike on and wait for me at the intersection of Raven Fork "man-way" with the Enloe Creek Trail.

I fished at this awesome spot for some time, and then, continuing down Raven Fork, I fished a little more. Before long I got to a point where I couldn't find the trail, and going on down the stream looked impossible.

Raven Fork is unique in that it has miles of large, house-sized boulders along the stream. Suddenly I got panicky, and started to crawl up the side of the mountain that seemed almost vertical on the side of the stream where I thought the trail was located. Desperately I sought the man-way. I kept crawling up the steep cliff, burdened by all the gear I was carrying. After what seemed like an eternity as I climbed and crawled up the mountain, I finally found the trail probably 150 foot above the stream. I flopped down on it, and lay there some time, relieved, and thanking God that I had found the trail. Finally I put on my hiking boots, got up, and backpacked the rest of the way back to our planned meeting point. I didn't do anymore fishing. Total relief came over me when I saw my mentor patiently waiting for me at the planned meeting point. Neither before nor since have I experienced that level of fear about getting lost in the forest. Getting lost in so remote an area certainly could have had dire consequences!

As we took Enloe Creek Trail to the top of Hyatt Ridge I related the experience to my mentor. Then we hit Hyatt Ridge Trail and took it down the other side of the mountain to Straight Fork Road, hiking back to Round Bottom Campground and to our car, thus completing the loop trail. It had been an exhilarating, yet scary backcountry experience for me. It taught me that hikers must stay together and never hike the backcountry alone.

On a sad note, several years later my mentor was killed on the Alum Cave Trail hiking up to Mount LeConte over the New Year's holiday. He was helping a group of Boy Scouts from Asheville. Apparently he slipped on an ice-covered rock and fell to his death. His ashes were sprinkled in the Smoky Mountain National Park that he loved so much. His love of nature was passed on to me as one small part of his legacy.

In later years I returned to the lower section of Raven Fork to fish with friends, but I will never be able to return to the Three Forks Pool and to the upper section of Raven Fork. However, God's creative beauty in that place will forever remain with me.

Roan Mountain Joy

My favorite hike on the Appalachian Trail (AT) is atop Roan Mountain. It is a unique area with much diversity. One can find Canadian forests of fir and spruce, New England hardwoods, and rhododendron gardens. Found there also are mountaintop meadows, called balds, with 360 degree, 50-mile views. One can see all of this and more within a fifteen-mile section of the AT. I think of it as Roan Mountain joy; a special place to reflect on planet Earth that God gave us the privilege to enjoy and responsibility to protect.

I have hiked or backpacked it quite a few times. I hope to hike at least some parts of it again. The first time, over thirty years ago, an Asheville friend took me there. I remember in particular descending from Roan High Knob to Carvers Gap through a magnificent Canadian-like forest of fir and spruce.

In recent years the balsam fir are being killed by an insect, balsam wooly adelgid, leaving many balsam fir tree skeletons standing. It reminds me of the dead saguaro cactus skeletons in the Sonora Desert of Arizona. Hopefully, the balsam fir will come back from the struggling seedlings growing on the forest floor.

This would be unlike the fate of the magnificent American chestnut tree, which was attacked by a fungus carried by imported ornamental Asian chestnut trees in about 1900. The fungus quickly spread throughout eastern United States, killing all American chestnut trees between about 1900 and 1945. Seedlings try to make a comeback, but they are killed by the blight before reaching maturity.

A US National Forest supervisor with whom I talked in April 2005 spoke of a new strain of American chestnut tree they are planting that seems to resist the fungus.

Unfortunately it will be fifty years before it will be known if it is successful.

Roan Mountain is likely named for the reddish tint of Roan High Knob in late June when the catawba rhododendron gardens are in full bloom. God is the sole gardener of the six to eight foot tall rhododendron plants covered with large pink and lavender flowers and separated from adjacent plants by grass.

It is one of the largest rhododendron gardens in the world. Many people drive to the garden in late June, and the parking lot is usually full then. Handicapped people enjoy a special path built for them. How I wonder at this nature garden that appears to be well tended.

After one of our hikes through the garden my wife and I backpacked to the AT, only a few hundred yards away, and hiked to the Roan High Knob shelter. Nobody else was on the trail or at the shelter. This shelter has the highest elevation of any along the entire AT. We had it all to ourselves and were glad we had warm sleeping bags even in late June. The next morning we backpacked down to Carvers Gap to enjoy the Canadian forests in the southern Appalachians.

Crossing the highway on the AT in Carvers Gap, heading north, is like being transported to the grasslands of Kansas and the Dakotas, except that instead of being on flat land the grasslands are on the top of the mountain ridges. These are known as balds. These meadows are on the ridges, with forests of hardwood below. Hiking is unique on the bald ridges with vistas to the left or the right as you walk, and valleys and views of mountain ridges many miles away. No one really knows the origin of the balds, except that they were here before the English arrived in the 1700's. They go on for miles. They are covered with several varieties of grasses, usually six to twelve inches tall. These balds are interspersed with small catawba rhododendron gardens at random in the meadows. Flame azalea bushes with their beautiful yellow-orange flowers are in bloom in June.

I have made the thirteen-mile hike from Carvers Gap to Highway US19E twice. The first time was day hiking with my wife, daughter, another couple and their daughter. The second time was backpacking with my wife, daughter, and four of her young friends.

The first trip made a very long day, including an unplanned side trip to Grassy Bald. We missed the AT white blaze marks, suddenly realizing we were following the blue blaze marks of a side trail. The two girls stood atop rocks on Grassy Bald and tried to whistle, but no sound came out because the wind was blowing so hard.

In spite of the wind I was glad for the side trip because we had a spectacular 360-degree, 50-mile view of the area from Grassy Bald. We could see the multiple parallel mountain ridges of Tennessee, resembling a giant's staircase! Turning 180 degrees, we could see small farms of North Carolina below us with rolling ridge tops beyond. Then turning 90 degrees more, we could view heavily forested Roan High Knob, and the path that we had followed from Carvers Gap. We wished that we could have seen it at sunset!

We imagined that we were participating in the "Sound of Music" story as we hiked along these balds on mountaintops named Round Bald, Jane Bald, Yellow Mountain, Little Hump Mountain and Hump Mountain - all part of Roan Mountain Highlands.

Hump Mountain provided another ideal spot to view the beautiful, surrounding mountains and valleys in all directions. The one exception to the awesome views was that of the intrusive condominiums atop Sugar Mountain, probably 40 miles away. Among the prominent mountains we could see Grandfather Mountain, with its facial profile, Beech Mountain where we had skied, and Mount Rogers, Virginia's highest mountain.

From Hump Mountain our hike was all down hill. This was hard on our knees and toes especially, since the ground was steep and rocky. It was now dusk. We hurried as fast as we could to get back to the car before dark. We barely made it! This hike with our friends will always bring back wonderful memories of an exhilarating experience.

The second trip from Carvers Gap to US19E, which we made several years later, was a backpacking trip. It took two days to make this trip. The first day we backpacked from Carvers Gap to Yellow Mountain Gap where we spent the night. The mountain views were excellent, with rhododendron and flame azalea still blooming in early July. We also had the good fortune to see the rare Gray's lily in bloom. It is a rare, reddish, six-petal, bell-like flower that is also found in New England.

The Yellow Mountain Gap Shelter was a uniquely refurbished barn with room in the loft to sleep at least twenty-five people. We had our supper and went to bed early, since we knew tomorrow would be a very long day. Another man shared the large loft with us that night, and he smelled very bad. We lined up our sleeping bags at the other end of the loft from him. The next morning he told us that a mouse ran across his bearded face during the night.

The next day we got an early start and hiked up Yellow Mountain, Little Hump Mountain, and Hump Mountain. After enjoying all the 360-degree, 50-mile views atop Hump Mountain again, we ate our lunch and lay in the grass to rest and view the sky.

Someone noticed dark clouds heading our way with faint thunder and lightning. Grabbing our packs and raingear, we started down Hump Mountain as fast as possible, since we were like seven lightning rods standing on top of the tallest mountain within about seven miles!

The rain started before we got down into the forest below. To our great relief it was just a scattered, summer thunderstorm that passed over quickly. We dropped twenty-five hundred feet in elevation in five miles from Hump Mountain, welcoming the sound of traffic on US19E, as this incredible trip was about to end.

Every hiking experience can provide the thrill of new discoveries as well as affording once again cherished views from another adventure on God's wonderful planet Earth. The haunting question is whether many of the pristine and unique lands of this Earth can be saved and protected so future generations can experience the same joy of hiking.

Deep Creek Trail in Early Spring

The Smoky Mountain National Park in the southern Appalachian Mountains is a wonderful place to backpack. I have had many backpacking trips in the Smokies, but this may be the most memorable. My wife and I did it with our daughter, Ginger, and her best girlfriend, Suzanne, and parents, Sherrill and Tony. The girls were on "spring break" their freshman year in high school. As parents, we were delighted that our daughters would want to do this with their parents at this age. It showed their maturing love of nature.

    We designed this as a point-to-point trip, driving to Deep Creek Campground to leave a car at the trail-end, then driving back up to the starting point at the Deep Creek Trailhead near Newfound Gap. This was a three-day, fourteen-mile trip down Deep Creek Valley. Due to the logistics of arranging the cars it was mid-afternoon before we started down the trail with our packs.

    Only two hundred yards down the trail we had our first surprise: a black bear eating berries off a tall bush. It was standing on its hind legs reaching to the top of the bush. We quietly watched for a while without being noticed. Continuing quickly on the trail while the bear was still eating the berries, we were thankful that it had not picked up the scent of the steaks we had in our backpacks.

    The first day's hike was about 4.5 miles down a very steep mountain. We reached the Poke Patch campsite in time to build a campfire, cook our steaks, eat supper and set up our tents. The sound of the rushing stream provided a relaxing background. Our last task before going to bed was to get the rest of our food in a sack and position it high up in a tree so bears couldn't reach it.

    The plan was to tie one end of a rope to the sack, then tie the other end to a rock. The trick was to throw the rock with rope attached over a limb high up in a selected tree. The rock with the rope attached fell back to earth allowing us to hoist the sack into the proper position high up in the tree and secure it there by tying the end of the rope to the trunk of the tree. The bag of food would dangle in mid-air, away from the bear's reach even if it climbed the tree.

Describing this procedure reminded me how I was given my "trail name." Trail names are descriptive names given to AT backpackers usually by their hiking companions based on some characteristic or experience of the hiker. My trail name is "One Rock Dick." Somehow I always seemed to be able to throw the rock, with rope attached, over the desired tree limb on the first attempt, thus allowing us to quickly hang our food out of the bear's reach. This was a very important skill with very limited use.

Since our tents were close to the stream, the lullaby of the water helped sleep come quickly. The stream's music also prevented us from hearing the bears that were prowling during the night. Fortunately, they couldn't reach our food high in the tree. However, the four men camped across the creek were not so fortunate. They had left their food in one of their packs and had not hung it in a tree. The pack had been completely demolished. Fortunately they were nearing the end of their trip and would not suffer from lack of food, only from the loss of one backpack.

Our second day was a difficult hiking day because, as the stream's name describes, it is deep! Crossing the tributaries and the main stream with backpacks was an adventure made more difficult because of the early spring rains. Since the upper two-thirds of the trip had no footbridges at the stream crossings, we would take off our hiking boots and either go barefooted or wear sneakers across the cold flowing water while wearing our packs. Safely across, we would dry our feet, put our boots back on, and continue the hike. It went slowly, but it was a fun challenge.

At one tributary a log had fallen across the stream making a natural bridge about eight feet above the water. So instead of wading, we decided to walk across the stream on the log. Tony set up a taut rope between trees on either side of the tributary, which we used for balance as we crossed with our packs. We all made it across successfully with our backpacks!

Sherrill wanted to photograph Suzanne crossing the tributary on the log with her backpack, so she asked her to go back to the other side. When she was crossing back on the log for the third time, the rope slackened. She lost her balance, falling backwards on top of her pack in the tributary. She was not injured, but got thoroughly soaked!

The second night at Nick's Nest Branch we camped in luxury under a canopy of huge pine and spruce trees with a plush carpet of needles underneath. It was a large area, which we shared with only squirrels and birds. Our ample supper was cooked over another campfire, superbly built by Tony. Black beans and rice with cheese was the main course followed by toasted-marshmallows, chocolate bars and graham crackers, otherwise know as "smores."

It seems that logs played an important role in this backpacking trip. We finally got downstream far enough to cross Deep Creek on hand-built, single-log bridges with a single handrail. However, one in particular is memorable. This one was about twenty feet above Deep Creek, which was now rather wide. Sherrill and I are both afraid of heights, so we shimmied across this log on our butts, wearing our backpacks. The others nonchalantly walked across holding onto the small wooden handrail, which was bolted to the log.

We arrived at our car late that afternoon exhausted, but exhilarated. A hard rain set in so we decided to stay in a small motel at the trailhead instead of tent camping that night.

The fourth day we rented inflated inner tubes, and floated and careened down the lower part of Deep Creek above the campground. The tubes had a wooden piece across the bottom to sit on. These seats were quite helpful with the bumpy, exciting ride down the creek. The upper part of this section was particularly scary, at least for the adults. As we realized later, only a few of the more daring people at the park started at the upper end of the float trip.

On our last night we rented a motel room in the town of Cherokee, and were given free tickets to see the dress rehearsal performance of the play "Unto these Hills." This performance was for the local people. The next morning in the parking lot of our motel we had the good fortune to meet Robert Bushyhead, well-known Native American (deceased 2001) who played the part of the medicine man in the play the previous night. Tony vividly remembers his reciting verses from Psalm 121 in the Cherokee language that starts with the words "I lift up my eyes to the hills – where does my help come from? My help comes from the Lord, the Maker of heaven and earth."

Besides being an actor he was a pastor and linguist, who worked to preserve the Kituhwa dialect of the Eastern Band of Cherokees. We knew none of this when we invited him to our motel room to talk with the girls in 1990. They particularly loved learning from him about the Cherokee language, legends, and stories. He gave each of them a poster of himself, which had been used by the Cherokee Nation as their poster for the Knoxville World's Fair. The poster stressed the Cherokee Nation's love of this world's natural resources and their desire to preserve them. Those two posters are still hanging in Ginger's room at our home and at Suzanne's room at Sherrill and Tony's home after all these years.

The exhilaration and serenity shared during these days with good friends is unforgettable. But now my mind drifts forward in time to June 1994, and to the tragic death of eighteen-year-old Suzanne, and the unbearable sorrow and pain Sherrill and Tony will always feel with her loss. Now as I write this, millions of people in South Asia are suffering from the deaths of over two hundred thousand of their relatives and friends caused by the Sumatra tsunami disaster.

Why, God, do these tragedies occur? I feel some of Sherrill and Tony's pain even today. I also feel the Sumatra tsunami victims' pain. Almost all human beings respond in a positive way to provide comfort to the victims. I have learned from this that life is precious, yet fragile, like crossing a beautifully forested mountain stream on a log. The odds are that we are all going to get wet at some time along life's path.

I will always cherish the memory of that wonderful week that is bound so intimately with tragic loss and unfulfilled dreams. With tears in my eyes I wonder in the depth of my soul about life's mysteries, while reliving the hiking trip along Deep Creek Trail in early spring.

Mount Rogers Highlands

The Mount Rogers Highlands is a wonderful area to explore along the AT in southwestern Virginia. I have made two backpacking trips in this area with family and friends, and hope to hike there again. Among its attractive features are balds or meadows, especially at Rhododendron Gap where there is probably the largest number of catawba rhododendron bushes in the country.

It is forested predominately with fir and spruce at the highest elevations and northern hardwoods at somewhat lower elevations. Within the forests there are not as many distance views as one finds when hiking along Roan Mountain, but the biodiversity and geological formations are outstanding.

Our first backpacking trip was "spring break" of Ginger's senior year in high school. We had with us Ginger's friend and her parents as well as the girls' two boy friends for a total of eight. We planned to do a point-to-point backpacking trip, so we positioned one car at our planned end point and drove the other car to the start point at Elk Garden. As we drove up the mountain to the gap a fog became more and more dense and snow covered the ground. The snow became deeper as we ascended. It was the first week of April, and this was supposed to be spring!

We arrived at Elk Garden at about 4400 feet elevation, and began our hike by heading north through a bald area along the AT. Because of the dense fog it took forever to find the white blaze marks on rocks, showing the trail. A light drizzle soon changed to sleet and light snow. Snow already covered the ground to a depth of six to ten inches. Burdened with our backpacks it was difficult to hike up the steep trail.

It was about five miles to a newly built shelter, and on the way we skirted the summit of Mount Rogers, the highest peak in Virginia with an elevation of 5700 feet. We hiked at a rate of about one mile per hour and got to the shelter about dark. There was fog all the way. This first day was a physical and mental challenge for us, having never backpacked in snow.

The shelter was a log structure with two levels. We referred to it as the Mount Rogers Hilton, although its actual name is the Thomas Knob shelter. We climbed a ladder to the second level, which was enclosed on all sides. The quarters were barely adequate for all eight of us in a close-packed array.

As we got settled to go to bed two men and a woman arrived at the shelter. They had backpacked in from the opposite direction. Since there was no room for them on the upper level, they set up their tent in the open lower level of the shelter. They were not protected from the wind, as was the upper level. The wind howled throughout the night, but we were warm and comfortable in our "mummy" bags, indulging in the satisfaction of rest after total exhaustion.

The temperature was well below freezing by next morning. The other hikers convinced us that we should return the way we came because the snow was even deeper ahead at Rhododendron Gap.

While we were melting snow over the fire for a hot breakfast we were visited by some of the wild feral ponies that are found in the Mount Rogers Wilderness Area. We were delighted with the encounter and petted them, but wisely didn't give them the handout they were seeking.

After breakfast we hiked back the way we came as suggested by the other hikers, returning to the starting car at Elk Garden. We drove to pick up the second car, which was parked at the planned endpoint. We camped there that night and reassessed our plans.

The next day we drove to Grayson Highlands State Park, which adjoins Mount Rogers Wilderness Area. Our new plan was to do day hiking in this Park. The weather was much warmer and sunny for our hike up to Massie Gap on the AT. At that point we found more feral ponies eager for us to pet them and take their pictures.

We hiked along the AT to Wilburn Ridge, which was Ginger's favorite spot. She had written a song about it after an earlier trip. Wilburn Ridge is an absolutely beautiful ridge with rocks jutting upwards, and the views from there are outstanding.

Two days and a few miles can make a big difference in the weather conditions. Now it was sunny and much warmer, with no snow on the ground! We adults were lying in the grass relaxing and absorbing the warm sun after lunch while the kids were climbing the Wilburn Ridge rock outcroppings. Suddenly two Air Force jets on training exercises flew above us, and disrupted the serenity of Wilburn Ridge. As the planes made two passes overhead they were so low that we could see the pilots in them. This was an unexpected clash between the serenity of nature and the noise of human invention. Just two days earlier the circumstances had been just reversed. Then we had experienced nature's fury of howling wind and deep snow outside our shelter while we were nestled all snug in our high-tech sleeping bags.

The second backpacking trip in the Mount Rogers Highlands was several years later in the early fall. On this occasion my wife and I went with a Christian group named Wilderness Trail, Inc, whose purpose is to expose young people to outdoor experiences in a Christian environment. Their appropriate motto is "Be strong enough to carry your own burden; be compassionate enough to help others carry theirs."

On this trip we started from Highway 603 and backpacked the AT up Pine Mountain, completing our trip near Scales, so named because farmers used to weigh their cattle here before and after their summer months in the high country meadows.

During this trip we also hiked over to Rhododendron Gap that we had missed on the earlier trip. Although the gardens were not in bloom, they were impressive because of their sheer size. The hike was enjoyable, and even more so because we were with friends and the youth from our church. We hoped that it helped the youth experience the link between creation and the Creator that we had found in our experience, and helped them grow in their spiritual life.

North Georgia Uniqueness

My friend Randy (deceased, 2007) and I had hiked in the Red River Gorge of Kentucky, but had never taken a backpacking trip on the AT together. So we decided that before we got any older, we should just do it. In early May 1998 we took the AT from near Springer Mountain, Georgia, to Neel's Gap, Georgia. It was a thirty-mile, five-day and four-night trip.

We began the hike with the weather threatening. A hail and rain storm developed just before dark. This was my first experience hiking on squishy marbles. The Stover Creek shelter was full when we arrived so we had to set up our tent in a light drizzle after dark.

After the first night's difficulty, the trip was ideal. It was the peak of the wildflower season for this elevation. Without foliage on the trees we could enjoy many gorgeous views below.

The second night we spent at Hawk Mountain shelter, a double-decker shelter that we shared with others. Some were thru-hikers and others were section-hikers, as we were. It was a pleasure to get acquainted with congenial strangers. Randy's birthday fell on this day, and I had secretly brought a cupcake and a candle as well as a small bottle of wine for a celebration. We all sang happy birthday to him as I lit the candle on the cupcake.

The third night we tent camped right by the AT with two of the thru-hikers we had gotten acquainted with the day before. It seemed they were hiking at about our pace.

A few other unique experiences occurred on this trip. First, we had lunch at Wood's Hole shelter, which had just been built by the Georgia AT Club (GATC), and it had a privy! I don't ever remember staying at an AT shelter with a privy when hiking there twenty to thirty years ago. So now we have more of the comforts of home. The privy is designed like a miniature shelter with the front open. So while you are seated, you can look out on a spectacular view of the mountains and the valley below. Also, to make it feel more like home, the GATC had attached a flower box with various wildflowers in it to the side of the privy below a false window. It was a friendly human touch amidst the natural beauty.

Randy and I spent the fourth night at the Blood Mountain rock shelter. Mice were our only inside company. In early evening we stood on a prominent boulder by the shelter. We could see for a great distance, but one of the sights was ominous – thunderstorm clouds moving towards us.

Soon it began to rain, and as we were trying to go to sleep the thunder and lightning started. The storm lasted for hours! It was frightening because the thunder sounded at the same time the lightning flashed. I could hear crackling along with the thunder, and the smell of ozone filled the air. We were at the highest point within fifty miles. Here we were secure from the rain, but not from the lightning. It was a long night, but the next morning the sun was shining brightly, and after breakfast we packed up for the steep descent of Blood Mountain to Neel's Gap.

Another "first" for me occurred while I was outside the Blood Mountain shelter waiting for Randy to finish getting ready for our departure. As many people know, among the wonderful aspects of hiking and backpacking are the unique people you meet along the trail and at the shelters. They can have such different views of life, although traveling the same path.

I met a man with a unique perspective coming up Blood Mountain southbound on the AT while I was waiting for Randy. We talked for a while. He gave me his business card with his trail name: "Long Haul Paul." It included his total mileage as of that day, May 8, 1998, of 10,700 miles. His goal was to hike the perimeter of the continental United States alone by July 4, 2000.

Paul must have loved logistics. His equipment included a pick-up truck with a camper top. He used the pick-up truck to pull a car on a trailer to the end point for that day's hike. He would then drive the pick-up pulling the empty trailer to the start point for that day's hike, and hike between the two vehicles during the day.

After completing the day's hike, he would drive the car back to the day's starting point, eat supper and sleep in his pick-up truck with camper top. The next day he would repeat this procedure. I estimate that it required over 600 repeats to accomplish his goal. Paul's hiking goal was quite different from mine, and that demonstrates the uniqueness of individuals. I recently looked up "Long Haul Paul" using Google, and discovered that he was honored in 2002 by his hometown of Bellflower, California, for completing his ambitious goal on Labor Day weekend of 2002, a trip totaling almost 15,000 miles!

As Randy and I backpacked down Blood Mountain, I was in the lead and telling about my experience meeting "Long Haul Paul." Once I turned my head to repeat something I had said, and to my amazement I saw a group of four pink lady slippers blooming near the trail! A euphoric feeling came over me! They are my favorite wildflower, and we hadn't seen one on the whole trip. What a fitting climax to this wonderful five-day backpacking trip that we completed a short time later at Neel's Gap.

My posthumous congratulations go to "Long Haul Paul" (deceased, 2004) on his unbelievable hiking achievement.

White Blaze Marks and Our Spiritual Journey

All hikers and backpackers who walk any part of the 2,175 miles of the Appalachian Trail (AT) between Springer Mountain, Georgia, and Mount Katahdin, Maine, know that there are rectangular white blaze marks along the trail. Their purpose is to assure you that you are on the right pathway.

The white blaze marks are painted on trees in the forests, on rocks in the grasslands, and on fence posts where stiles are built to provide a means to cross a fenced pasture. They are two inches wide by six inches high, large enough to be seen from a distance. If the path location is obvious, the white blaze marks are farther apart. Where there may be uncertainty about the trail direction, they are much closer together.

If there is a side trail crossing coming up soon, there will be a warning sign designated by two white blaze marks, one above the other with a two-inch spacing. These double blaze marks caution the hiker to beware not to take the side trail by mistake. Side trails that connect to the AT are usually marked with blue blaze marks the same dimensions as those on the AT. Since hikers are both northbound and southbound, the white blaze marks must be painted on both sides of a tree or an adjacent tree so hikers going both ways are assured that they are on track.

Many times hikers like myself have missed seeing a white blaze mark, and continuing on, have asked the others in the group, "Has anyone seen a white blaze mark recently?" If the answer is "No," it can seem like an eternity until one is spotted and the anxiety level dissipates. What seems easy on a clear day can be almost impossible on a foggy, rainy, or snowy day, when one can see only a short distance ahead.

Our own spiritual journey may be likened to hiking the AT. The two white blaze marks, one above the other, along our spiritual journey are there to warn our conscience that we may be tempted to try one of those blue blaze side trails just ahead. The warning is obvious: beware, and stay on the right path! God has marked the way, but we have free will to go off on a side trail if tempted by a "thrill." However, God will forgive us, if we ask, and will help guide us back to the pathway.

The AT may seem long, but the trip and reaching the end provide us with good memories and insight. Following the true path of life brings joy as well as pain, but the reward is to live in relationship with God. Following the divinely revealed path is its own reward with eternal life as a bonus.

If someone with the group starts to lag behind, or becomes disinterested and stops, another hiker can go back by following the white blaze marks, find them and help them move forward. Perhaps they need us to carry some of their load. It may be a foggy day for them on their personal journey, and they cannot find their way by themselves. We are instructed by the well-known parable of the Good Samaritan. Briefly stated, the parable tells us that some religious people passed by without helping a fellow countryman who had been robbed and injured along the road. Then a Samaritan, a member of the despised minority, helped the injured man. This parable is an inspiration to help others carry their load and bind up their wounds when needed.

Through technological developments for backpacking we have lighter weight backpacks, improved hiking boots, breathable rain suits, hiking poles, freeze-dried foods, and global positioning system (GPS) devices to make our AT journey easier.

In the dense fog that we sometimes experience in our lives prayer is our guidance system to discern God's indicated pathway. God is there for us as the GPS is there for the AT hiker. At times a well-worn path, one that our culture has established, but which leads us away from the true pathway, can fool us. If we learn that we have been misled, we may be able to return to the right pathway through divine communication, help from others, or through our own seeking.

The AT is rerouted occasionally. This may result in confusion as to which way is the correct way. This can happen if some of the old weathered white blaze marks are not removed. Likewise, in our spiritual journey it sometimes isn't clear which way to go, so we must listen for the answer from the ever-present God. However, it is up to us to discern the answer.

In the spring of 2004 my wife and I were hiking up Wolfe Ridge Trail in the Twenty Mile Creek watershed of the Smokies. A young man caught up with us, and we started walking and talking with him. He was by himself, and had a unique goal for the day. He was using his GPS device to find the remains of an airplane that had crashed in the Smokies over twenty-five years ago. He told us that all the plane crashes in the Smokies have been documented as to their latitudinal and longitudinal coordinates. It was his hobby to hike to them and observe the remains. Then, suddenly, he told us goodbye, and headed up the mountainside where there was no trail to follow. He trusted that the GPS device would get him to his destination and back before darkness.

We also must trust that God is with us whether our life's journey takes us through easy or difficult times. Just as white blaze marks and the GPS device are guiding tools, God gives us the Holy Spirit, the Bible, and prayer to discern the pathway for our life. God is infinite, timeless, all knowing, and passionately loving. Those who honestly seek God will not be disappointed.

TROUT FISHING

*I've fished with all kinds of pretty little flies
And I plan to do so till the day I die.*

*If as they say, trout fishing is good for the soul,
Surely Heaven's streams will always run cold.*

Jimmy D. Moore

Trout Fisherman's Soul

Why does a trout fisherman walk for miles, burdened with equipment, and then wade in a cold rushing stream on slippery rocks? For some it is to see how many fish they can catch. For others it is the entomological delight of identifying the hatch coming off the water so as to select just the right fly to cast.

For me it is being in harmony with God's ecological system where catching a brook, brown, or rainbow trout on a dry fly is a wonderful bonus. Or perhaps it is just part of my trout fisherman's soul.

Trout streams in the southern Appalachians have names corresponding to flora and fauna native to the area. Names such as Eagle, Raven, Laurel, Sassafras and White Oak, and Cherokee names like Cataloochee, Oconalufte and Santeetlah. The streams have varied terrain including long pools flowing through meadows, cascading waterfalls, and everything in between. One sees house-sized boulders, impenetrable rhododendron, and tranquil stream settings to enjoy the beauty of nature.

Harmony with God's ecological system is my goal in trout fishing. So I fish in streams that have only wild, native-born trout. That limits the number of streams available to me because many trout streams are stocked with hatchery grown trout. The hatchery trout may be larger, but they aren't the scrappy fighters nor do they have the brilliant colors of the natives.

Most trout fishermen prefer fishing the stocked streams because they are more likely to be successful at catching more and larger trout. Also, many trout fishermen use wet flies and nymphs, which sink under water, and they are usually more successful catching trout than those who use only dry flies floating on the water surface. There are numerous perspectives on trout fishing in the southern Appalachians. My approach, dry fly fishing for native trout, represents only one such choice.

When dry fly fishing, I wade up the stream and try to imagine where the trout are safely waiting for their food to float downstream to them. I quietly study the pool, the main current through the pool, the riffles, the rocks sticking out of the water and those submerged. Since the water is so clear, it is important to be careful that my shadow is never on the water or the fish will be spooked.

Casting can be complicated because of the vegetation along the stream banks. I must estimate the distance to where I want my fly to land upstream from me. I need to be sure that the back cast won't reach the trees or rhododendron growing close to the stream, or overhanging behind me. Failure to do so can result in losing a fly. Many times an overhead cast is appropriate. But there are times when I must compromise using a side cast or a roll cast to avoid obstacles. After my initial study, I determine where to stand for the first cast so that the floating fly will appear natural as it floats downstream. After moving to the selected spot in the stream, I make new estimates of the target distance and the casting method. I cast upstream, and let the fly drift back towards me while I draw in the excess line with the opposite hand. This keeps the line straight. Thus I gain maximum reaction time to set the hook when there is a strike. It is most important to ensure that the fly appears to be floating freely down the stream.

Dry fly fishing for trout is my favorite method because for me there is nothing more exciting than watching a fly floating peacefully down the stream over riffles and through small pools and then seeing the water explode like a geyser. I feel a tingling thrill as I react to set the hook with the fly rod. A second later I feel the fly line and leader go taut, and I have hooked a fish! It may leap out of the water a couple of times, attempting to get off the hook as I bring the fly line toward me, keeping the leader taut. The more feisty ones may also try flashing across the pool or getting into fast water in an attempt to escape the hook. The encounter happens quickly, and I must be careful to keep my balance. I must not wade into water deeper than my waders, and I must keep the trout in the pool with the line and leader taut as I attempt to guide my prize into a net or to the stream bank.

After landing the trout, I measure its length quickly, to be certain that it's long enough to keep for cooking over tonight's campfire. If not, I gently return it to the stream for another day.

A day of trout fishing can be as tiring as snow skiing or white water canoeing. But the payoff is a sense of calmness and serenity. Trout fishing requires a partner for safety, but more important, sharing God's Earth with another human being is an added benefit that enriches a trout fisherman's soul.

Fishing for Trout and People

I have dry fly fished for trout roughly once a year for thirty-five years. Longevity doesn't make me an expert, for I have had to relearn casting each time. However, like bike riding, once you have learned the skill you can relearn it again rather quickly.

The streams, trout, and ambience are the same today as when I made my first cast. Fishing gear and footwear, however, have seen many technological advances over those years. I used to fish in sneakers with felt glued to the bottom for safer wading in the streams. Now I use stocking waders with boots that have felt bottoms, and I carry a walking stick to help keep my balance when wading on slippery rocks.

When I started trout fishing everyone used a nylon leader that tapered down to a small tip on which you tied the dry fly. This design was used to prevent the trout from seeing the leader, making it appear that the insect was floating freely down the stream. Now many trout fishermen use a fluorocarbon, tapered leader that has almost the same refractive index as water. This new leader has a high density causing it to break the water surface tension more quickly than nylon, thus eliminating the surface shadow of the leader. With these two characteristics, the new leader becomes invisible to the trout. The improved technology leads to safer and more productive trout fishing experiences.

To be a successful dry fly trout fisherman it is necessary to see the world from the trout's perspective, and to understand how they catch their food. I have learned to use several dry fly patterns, which I think the trout may want to eat. These flies have names like March Brown, Parachute Adams, Stimulator, Royal Wulff, and Light Cahill. They attempt to simulate the living insect hatch appearing on the water surface at that season. If I don't present the dry fly to the trout as they normally see it in their stream environment, they will ignore it. However, if I make a good cast, with the dry fly floating naturally down the stream over the trout, it will usually strike at it even if the fly doesn't imitate the real insects that are in the stream.

I first experienced this when my daughter and I were brook trout fishing on Laurel Fork in northwestern Virginia. We had caught a few on various dry flies. I came to the tail end of a long pool using a March Brown fly. With my first cast I had a big strike and landed a brookie. Moving upstream only a few yards I cast again and caught another. My luck continued until I had caught five nice brook trout in rapid succession, and released them all. The fly by now was in bad shape with part of the hackle missing. Hackle is made from waterproof neck feathers of a fowl that are wrapped around the hook to form the artificial dry fly that mimics a real insect.

I suggested that my daughter use my fly rod and start casting just above where I had caught the last fish. In ten to fifteen minutes she caught three more nice brook trout and released them. After all this action, much of the March Brown's hackle was missing, so we concluded that dry fly presentation is more important than fly condition!

On another occasion the importance of fly presentation was illustrated when a friend and I were fishing a large pool together below a waterfall. He was using a pink Parachute Adams and I was using a Stimulator. We both were catching fish at the same time. These dry flies we noted are distinctly different in color and appearance. The Parachute Adams has a grayish-brown body, black tail, black wings and a pink parachute. A parachute is a post of hackle that is tied to the metal fly shaft and sticks straight up when the fly is in the water. It is usually a color that contrasts with the water to make the fly easier for the fisherman to see. The Stimulator usually has a yellow and orange body, yellow tail, yellow wings, and no parachute. This suggests that the fisherman's skill at fly presentation to the trout is more important than the design of the fly.

Presentation is important in many other fields as well: consider politics, law, business, food preparation, and religion. Webster gives several related definitions: 1) the act of presenting, 2) something offered or given, and 3) a descriptive or persuasive account such as by a salesman.

I can remember an example when I was on a jury in which the prosecution's case was poorly prepared. I was frustrated that I could not stand up as the foreman of the jury and ask my own probing questions of the defendant. The defense attorney was very skilled, and emphasized in his closing presentation that the jury needed to acquit the defendant, if he wasn't proven guilty beyond a reasonable doubt. In my opinion the defendant was guilty, but I voted to acquit because of the phrase "beyond a reasonable doubt." The presentation of the prosecuting attorney was so poor that I had no other choice under the law.

There are many other examples of the importance of presentation. At fine restaurants food is more appealing because of skillful presentation on the plate. In business a high compliment to a salesman's presentation skills would be that "he could sell refrigerators to Eskimos." In religion dedicated disciples and scholars of different faiths have passed down the scriptures first through word of mouth and then through written narratives and today ministers present it orally in inspiring messages.

As a follower of Jesus Christ I believe God's truths are revealed in the Bible. The Holy Scriptures of the Torah, Qur'an, and Hindu and Buddhist writings all have some of God's truths in them. God, the Divine Being, is known by different names in these religions such as Yahweh, Allah, and Ultimate Reality. It seems much more important how we live in response to God, than what name we call God.

Eternal truths were presented or communicated to our ancestors starting about five millennia ago, and they apply to us today as then in spite of the incredible technological advances and cultural changes during this span of time. Belief in Jesus Christ as the only Son of God, who showed us how to live, has not been modified in two millennia.

The trout fisherman uses skill to attract the hungry trout and God desires to attract all of us who are hungry for the truth. We have free will to choose whether to accept God or not, just as the trout can take the dry fly or not when the fisherman presents the fly to the fish.

Through the ages God has used different presenters to reach us including the Patriarchs, Judges, Kings, Prophets, and his only Son. Billions of us have been led to faith in the one God through the Holy Scriptures, Moses, Jesus, Mohammed, and God's many disciples. We live in many different life streams, and have different pleasures and storms, but our trust in God comes to all through our spiritual growth and prayer. Jesus selected four of His twelve disciples from among fishermen, and said that he would teach them to become "fishers of men"[1] or "to fish for people."[2] We have responsibility as Christian disciples to follow Jesus' two commandments: 1) to love God and 2) to love our neighbor as ourselves. Acting out our love of others may be the only presentation of God they ever see.

[1] Mark 1:17 (NIV)
[2] Mark 1:17 (NRSV)

Fishing Smoky Mountain Gems with a Good Friend

The pure spring water, the raindrops, and the snowflakes that fall on the Smoky Mountain slopes flow ever-downward uniting pairs of rivulets time and time again until they grow large enough to form a mountain stream. These mountain streams, to most hikers, are the gems of the Smokies. Their formation is analogous to a genealogist's family tree with life branching from our ancestors, generation after generation to create you and me.

There are many of these beautiful streams in the Smokies, and I have been fortunate to have either walked along or waded in sections of many of them. They differ strikingly, but they are all a delight. They saturate my senses!

Envision: on a sunny day the crystal-clear water moving slowly through a long pool where you can see the rocks on the bottom, six feet below. Then see the color of the surface water change from clear and bright in the sunlight to dark green as the water flows under the shadows of the overhanging rhododendrons.

Suddenly the water flows over the lip of the pool, down a cascading section of white water and foam sparkling in the sun's rays. Beyond the cascades the stream slows down, but it flows over and around rocks. The water color constantly changes as it flows from sunlight to shadows, riffles to whirlpools, and to calmer sections. The varied sounds of the flowing water in a mountain stream should not be missed either. Listen to the thunderous sound of a waterfall then to the dainty harmonies of water spilling over a riffle and around a rock. It reminds you of Handel's "Water Music Suite" with its many different orchestral sounds and movements.

You might describe the development of a friendship as having more and more enjoyable common experiences and perspectives. Each person will sacrifice and compromise, thus creating a deeper relationship over time. This happened to Brad and me as we initially developed a friendship through our professional work in the early 1980's.

Then we discovered that we both loved to trout fish. We also found we shared a mutual frustration because there weren't any native trout in the Kentucky streams: only hatchery grown trout. Brad had trout fished for native trout in his home state of New York; I had done the same while I lived in Asheville, North Carolina. I told him about the wild, native trout streams I had fished in the Smoky Mountain National Park. These streams were less than five hours from our homes.

Brad was convinced that we should try these streams. So we made plans for our first trip, choosing to combine backpacking with trout fishing over a long weekend in April. With us on that trip were his two sons and my two daughters. That first trip was quite a daring expedition because our children were in elementary and middle school that year. We chose to fish Big Creek on this first trip because the trail followed right along the stream all the way to the Walnut Bottoms campsite. There were no large elevation changes during the five-mile backpacking trip, making it easier for the kids to carry a share of the camping equipment.

Big Creek is spectacular with many large, clear, glass-like pools where trout can be spotted. We stopped at several of these, and made a few casts, but the trout weren't interested in our offerings. The sight and sound of Mouse Creek Falls dropping into Big Creek were memorable.

It took quite a while to get to the campsite, and to set up our three tents. We started fishing on Gunter Fork, a small tributary, but caught nothing that afternoon. It was exciting for both Brad and me to be trout fishing again. It was the first time in quite a few years for both of us.

We were the only people at the campsite. On Saturday we fished the main stream and caught enough rainbows so all of us had at least a taste of trout cooked over the campfire. The younger kids enjoyed playing in the stream more than trout fishing, but that was fine because they were learning the love of God's Earth. On Sunday we packed up our camping gear and backpacked out successfully. We stopped only long enough to try to catch those lazy trout in several crystal-clear, stationary pools. Our first trout fishing trip was a wonderful and exciting event for all of us. The trip also provided the opportunity to get to know my friend better, and in new ways, outside the work environment.

Following that successful trip, Brad and I decided to make it an annual event. We would go to the Smokies in April or May to backpack, trout fish, and enjoy each other's company. We must have made about twelve of these pilgrimages over a fifteen-year period.

While backpacking and trout fishing for native rainbows and browns along these marvelous streams, I also got to enjoy another passion of mine – spring wildflowers in bloom. In the early years one to four of our children went with us, but as they left home it was just Brad and I on these outings. Our friendship grew stronger over the years, reinforced by our sharing in work projects as well.

Except for our first trip to Big Creek on the North Carolina side of the Smokies, we fished the streams on the Tennessee side in the early years since they were closer to our homes in Kentucky. Each year we picked a new stream to explore. These included all three forks of the Little River and some tributaries; Abrams Creek including the remote, off trail Horseshoe Bend downstream from Cades Cove; and Porter Creek. I have a vivid recollection of our fishing Horseshoe Bend of Abrams Creek in the bright afternoon sun with the dazzling reflections from the water. It must have mesmerized both the rainbow trout and us, for we caught quite a few. It was an exhilarating feeling with only Brad and me privileged to enjoy this gem of a stream that afternoon.

Experience taught us that the difficulty of getting to the stream varies considerably. Sometimes it is relatively easy to get into the streams through the trees, and wade while fishing. On other streams it is an exhausting challenge even to get in or out of a stream. I will always remember our fishing a section of Porter Creek as a day trip. We decided to fish a remote section requiring a descent from the trail of more than a hundred feet in elevation to get into the stream. We chose to do it since most people wouldn't make the effort. Thus we would be more likely to catch some nice rainbows.

Despite the struggle to get to the stream, it was a wonderful adventure. Exploring and wading the stream required climbing over or going under trees that had fallen across the stream.

As anticipated, we caught some beautiful, intensely colored, native rainbows. However, getting back up to the trail after several hours of fishing was another matter! We were exhausted when we got back to the car. A memorable part of this trip was mentoring Brad's son as to where to make his cast. He placed the fly just below a very small waterfall. We saw the calm water explode, and shared his excitement as he landed a gorgeous rainbow.

We also fished the forks and tributaries of the Little River. There I landed the largest native rainbow trout I ever caught in the Smokies. It was on the cascading ledges of

Fish Camp Prong, and it was not the normally accepted way to catch a trout using a dry fly. It was pure luck, and happened when I cast my fly into a little pool where the swirling water submerged it. I couldn't see the fly in the frothing water, but I kept the line taut as I was bringing it back. I noticed the leader suddenly go zipping across the pool. I first thought it was caught on something submerged in the pool, but I kept the line and leader taut. The next thing I knew the leader darted the other way across the pool. I knew then that I had a fish! I was a long time landing it, and lucky to do so, since in all the excitement I slipped and fell, but managed to keep the line taut. Remarkably, I landed a beautiful rainbow! It made a savory supper that evening!

After we had fished the Tennessee streams in the Smokies, we decided to backpack and fish other North Carolina streams. We had already fished Big Creek, so now, over time, we added Bradley Fork, Forney Creek, Deep Creek, and Noland Creek. Each had its special charm.

Brad and I made another trip to Big Creek. This time it was just the two of us and we saw a lot of bear activity although we didn't see any bears. A mother and two cubs had climbed the tree above where other campers were tenting the night before we arrived.

Later that day we had an interesting talk with a park ranger who told us the bears are becoming more skilled at getting hikers' food despite the best plans to thwart them. He had seen a bear tight-rope-walk between two trees to get the food pack. He had also seen a bear climb the slender steel bear poles, and we witnessed the pack remnants there to prove it!

The ranger had walked to the campsite that day to see if he could prevent the bear from climbing the pole by putting axle grease on it. We had no problem the next two nights with our packs that were on the bear pole, so we know that the experiment was successful for two nights. We also put our food in a plastic bag and hung it over a limb high up in a relatively small tree. The bears didn't get that either.

I can vividly remember another event during this trip. When we were hiking back to the car we stopped at a small pool. I intended to make at least one cast into the pool. Sunlight was on the pool. The fly hit the water accompanied by a big explosion. I tried to set the hook, but missed the fish. The fly, leader, and a very fine mist of water droplets came flying high off the pool. The scene had the appearance of many sparkling stars shining in the night sky. It was the spectacular result of the sunlight reflecting off these miniature lenses. At that special moment, I felt that time had stopped. I could absorb this peaceful experience. It was an epiphany for me of God's magical creation. I have replayed this visual experience in my mind many times through the years!

After all these years of fishing in the Smokies with Brad, I have learned that you really don't need to have a lot of flies with you, especially not a lot of different kinds. When I was younger I thought lots of flies were necessary because you do lose them in the overhanging rhododendron and trees. I thought it would be terrible to run out of flies before I was ready to stop fishing. Of course, a major reason these streams are such gems of nature is because of the beauty of the vegetation that surrounds them, so I wouldn't complain about losing flies.

On one of our annual trout fishing pilgrimages up Forney Creek, I was sitting on a rock in the middle of the stream putting a new fly on my leader. In the excitement of getting ready to fish again, I dropped my little aluminum fly box in the creek. It landed like a perfect little boat, and went floating down the creek. There was no way that I could catch it, so I called to Brad downstream to help. He couldn't hear me over the sound of the rushing water. There went a lifetime supply of special flies down the creek towards Fontana Lake. I learned "don't put all your flies in one basket." But I discovered that there was a new dry fly recently developed that was much easier to see as it floated down the stream. It was called a Parachute Adams. I started using them very successfully, and got over the loss of my collection on Forney Creek.

Safety is a subject that we always kept in mind on our trips. We always included a first aid kit. In all these trips we never saw a snake when climbing in or out of a stream, nor did we ever see a bear or lose our food or backpacks to a bear. However, on one of our trips I had an unexpected challenge. It also proved Brad's friendship. We backpacked from Elkmont Campground up Little River to the Rough Creek campsite, which was 5.5 miles.

Again there was no one else at this campsite. After we set up camp, we started to fish, but within an hour I fell into the stream. I always fall several times in a long weekend, and this time, I put out my right hand to break the fall. My hand with most of my weight on it hit a sharp vertical rock submerged in the stream. The rock cut about a 1.5-inch gash in the palm of my hand. I bled profusely. It was scary. Fortunately, Brad wasn't far away, and we walked back to camp where he was able to bandage it and stop the bleeding.

Now it was dusk, and we knew we couldn't backpack out before darkness so we decided to spend the night. It was obvious that my hand needed attention. It was also obvious we couldn't do anything about it that night. It was a very long night. We backpacked out the next morning and went to a nearby hospital where they said that it was too late to stitch up the wound.

    We came on home, and Brad never displayed any disappointment over our ruined trip. It was a vivid example that taught us never to go to a remote area alone. I shudder to think of how it might have gone without Brad.

    These wonderful streams of the Smoky Mountains are marvelously relaxing, but also challenging. The relaxation and serenity come from just being in the outdoors in such a magnificently beautiful place with a good friend that also enjoys God's wonderful creation. These days are successful simply because one is there in nature at its best. If you don't catch a fish or even get a strike, but are sharing it with a friend, it is tremendously rewarding. I will always remember my friendship with Brad that grew stronger throughout the years while sharing the experiences of backpacking and trout fishing.

Big Snowbird Brookies

Randy (deceased, 2007) and I reflected on the serenity, emotional healing, and excitement that we both experienced in nature when backpacking, wildflower hiking, or trout fishing in the southern Appalachian Mountains. As Randy would say, "I'm home!" For us these experiences evoked a feeling of God's presence. I will always be grateful for the mentors that headed me along this pathway over thirty-seven years ago.

On a day in May 2001, we hiked along Big Snowbird Creek in the western North Carolina Mountains near Robbinsville, and vowed to return to this place to fish for southern native brook trout. The local people refer to brook trout as "specks," I suppose because of the small, light colored spots on a dark green background on their upper body. They are a beautiful fish with reddish orange underbody and red lower fins that complement their dazzling surroundings.

That day in 2001 we had been fishing for rainbow trout on a section upstream from "The Junction" (an old logging railroad junction). The brookies live in the headwaters and have been there since time immemorial, a gift from God. The southern and northern brook trout are the only native trout species that survive in the southern Appalachian Mountains. Non-native rainbow and brown trout were stocked in these streams starting about one hundred years ago because the brook trout population became dramatically reduced due to the extensive logging in the area. The "law of unintended consequences" resulted. The more aggressive rainbows took over the lower portions of the mountain streams and in many of the streams the brook trout became extinct.

Brook trout represented to us the precious, primal aspect of nature that we wanted to experience and preserve. So we eagerly anticipated a soul-satisfying experience away from the noise and rush of our culture. Tuesday after Memorial Day, 2003, we backpacked from the trailhead at "The Junction" along Big Snowbird Creek Trail to fish for brookies. Occasionally, remnants of the old narrow gauge railroad bed could be seen along the way to the confluence of Sassafras and Big Snowbird Creeks.

Sassafras Creek is a tributary in the Big Snowbird Creek watershed. We set up our campsite at the confluence of the two streams in a small, level clearing among the trees. The sun shone brightly where it penetrated the dense, late May foliage. This afternoon we caught plenty of rainbow trout on pink Parachute Adams dry flies. We kept what we needed for supper, charbroiling them on forked sticks over our campfire, and eating them with our fingers. They were delicious!

Anticipation of tomorrow did not keep sleep from arriving quickly under our nylon tarp. I awakened in the night and marveled at the myriad of brightly shining stars in the pitch-black sky: a good weather sign for dry fly fishing.

The next day's challenge was to catch southern native brook trout whose habitat has become limited to upstream of the first major waterfall. The aggressive rainbows couldn't encroach on the specks territory above Big Snowbird Creek and Sassafras Creek waterfalls unless they could fly! This was to become a day I shall always remember. Our preparation for the day included packing our lunch and a water bottle with a filter cap. The journey of discovery started with a hike, in wading boots, up Sassafras Creek Trail to the waterfall. We stopped to rest while absorbing the beauty of the cascading waterfall.

We did not tarry long, because the brookies were above the waterfall. Sassafras Creek is a small crystal clear stream that is relatively easy to wade, but difficult to cast because of the rosebay rhododendron and deciduous tree canopy. We began catching brook trout using pink Parachute Adams and Stimulator dry flies. Unlike rainbows, which are usually caught below riffles or in fast water, the brook trout were waiting in small calm pools for their food to float down to them. This makes the trout's strikes even more spectacular. The fish were too small to keep for supper, but the ambience and joyful experience were our main rewards.

Now was the time to fish for the Big Snowbird Creek brook trout. Hiking the long and steep trail to the top of the ridge that separated Sassafras Creek from Big Snowbird Creek was tougher than expected. Two surprising delights on the trek to the ridge top were the largest maple tree I'd ever seen and two maroon-purple, Vasey's nodding trillium. The latter has the largest flower in the entire trillium genus.

Hiking from the ridge down into the valley was a cakewalk, by comparison, and with wading sticks, and no backpack, Big Snowbird Creek was easy to wade. Finding the trail on the other side of the stream, we expected to turn directly downstream, but instead went uphill some distance from the stream through a thick forest.

After about a five-minute walk Randy thought he could hear roaring water. He peered through the dense trees and barely made out white water below. Then we came upon a steep side trail that finally led us down the mountainside. Suddenly we arrived at one of the most beautiful places I had ever seen: Middle Falls of Big Snowbird Creek sparkling in the sun with a large, mist-covered pool below! It was a large open area; unbelievable after all the narrow trails we had traversed. Climbing up on a large boulder, we ate lunch and absorbed the beauty of this spot with our senses, minds, and souls. It was a mystical experience for my friend and me to share even before we started fishing.

My lunch concluded, I suggested that I get some practice making long casts into the big pool while he finished his lunch. We had been restricted to short casts and roll casts on Sassafras Creek because of the tunnel of rhododendron and deciduous trees that had enclosed us.

Middle Falls of Big Snowbird Creek is the second waterfall upstream, so there should be brookies in this large pool. On the third practice cast I had a big strike on a Stimulator dry fly, and in a couple of minutes I had landed an eight-inch brook trout, which was large enough to keep for tonight's supper. It was beautiful with its spots, red fins, and reddish orange underside. I cast again in the same area as previously, where the water was flowing out of the left side of the pool at the boundary between sun and shade. I got another strike, but missed the fish. Casting two more times I had two more strikes and landed two more specks.

I called to Randy, "come fish this pool right now!" We fished the large pool side-by-side, which is unbelievable because it will usually spook the fish, but we both continued to catch specks. In an hour we had caught more than a dozen fish with five large enough for supper. Moving away from the large pool, we briefly fished above Middle Falls. We caught a couple more specks, but reluctantly stopped fishing this beautiful stream in order to get back to our campsite in time to cook and eat before dark.

We had a choice of two routes for returning to our campsite downstream on Big Snowbird Creek. One involved fording the creek ten times without much climbing. That sounded tiring and time consuming. The second alternative, and the one we chose, was to ascend on a trail to another ridge above the creek. It was another steep trail, and we were getting tired. We hiked along the ridge high above the creek, and when we descended we came to a group of unoccupied campsites and a bridge across the stream. After following several dead-end trails we crossed the bridge, and discovered that the trail continued on the other side. Continuing on downstream, we saw the cascading Bill Falls, which is the first falls on Big Snowbird Creek, but it was not nearly as dramatic as Middle Falls. Hiking rapidly we arrived back at our campsite at 7:00 pm. There still was nobody else at our campsite, and then we realized that we hadn't seen anyone along the entire loop hike that day.

That morning I had discovered a campfire grill that someone had left behind at the campsite, so we cleaned it, and used it to charbroil the trout. It took less time to cook on the grill since we could cook them all together. The brook trout tasted even better than the rainbow trout from the previous night. This had been an outstanding day! We had taken a risk by making it such a long day, including hiking seven miles over two ridges in addition to wading and fishing. I don't ever remember having a better day!

We finished our meal and cleaned up for the early nightfall in this deep valley. Needless to say we slept well that night, that is, until light rain started to fall about 4:00 am. It eventually turned into a heavy downpour before daylight. During the night we got the bottoms of our sleeping bags wet, having slid out from under the nylon tarp without realizing it. Fortunately the rain stopped, so we had our breakfast, packed-up our wet gear, and cleaned up the site. Nothing could dampen the God-connected experience that Randy and I had as we backpacked out that morning to his van.

We drove across the Cherohala Skyway to a magnificent view of Big Snowbird Creek watershed from near Hooper Bald, and on into Tennessee to fish another trout stream. We took with us eternal memories of the ambience of Big Snowbird Creek and its brookies.

REFLECTING

*By three methods we learn wisdom:
First, by reflection, which is the noblest;
second, by imitation, which is the easiest;
and third by experience, which is the bitterest.*

Confucius

Appalachian Friendship

The vast majority of the people that we meet at shelters or along a trail are pleasant and respectful of each other and the environment. The diversity of people's lives and occupations, and the conversations that result can be fascinating. With this diversity comes the surprising commonality of loving the beauty and challenges of the natural environment.

As I recall my many experiences hiking in the Appalachians that have helped me to grow in my relationship with God and to feel more in harmony with God's beautiful Earth, I am suddenly infused with feelings of peacefulness and serenity. However, it is hard to imagine experiencing God's wonderful creation without a companion to share it with. Many of my long-lasting friendships have resulted or have been reinforced by a common love of God and nature.

These friends also practice Jesus' second commandment of loving your neighbor as yourself. We men don't always express our love for each other verbally, but just know the feelings are mutual. In some cases a common interest has been wildflowers; in others it has been hiking or backpacking. For some of us it has been trout fishing. Occasionally it has been all, or different combinations of these.

Unfortunately, there are a few uninformed or indifferent people out on the trail who leave their trash behind at the AT shelters or campsites, and generally mistreat the environment. I suspect they have those same attitudes in other parts of their lives as well. One of my friends always picks up the trash left by these people and packs it out with him. He is a superb example of going beyond the "Leave No Trace" motto for backpacking.

Most everyone you spend the night with in an AT shelter treats each other as family, and shares stories, food and gear. On one backpacking trip we forgot the rain shield for our tent, and someone we met on the trail had an extra tarpaulin that he insisted that we take. We used it the rest of that AT trip on nights that we tent camped.

We met two solo hikers who had started from Springer Mountain. They were backpacking about the same speed as we were, so we tented with each other or shared the AT shelter with them a few nights. Thus our original pair became a foursome, which added to our perspective and pleasure on that backpacking trip. They both hoped, when they retired, to be more ambitious in their hiking. They planned to see how far they could hike along the AT, with a goal of reaching the end at Mount Katahdin in Maine.

We don't know if either of them made it, but we are sure that they were in better physical and mental shape no matter how far they got on their trips. One of them wanted to rest for several days before continuing northbound. In AT jargon the days of rest are called "zero days" since you don't hike any AT miles those days. Since our car was parked at Neel's Gap, the next road crossing, we offered to take him to a motel nearby. He gladly accepted. Thus we were able to drop him off at a motel so he could get several good nights' sleep in a real bed, and we returned home.

One excellent feature of the AT shelters is a logbook that is kept there for all hikers to use. It is used to communicate or inform others for many different reasons. In a way it is like a hand-written, hard copy of an internet "chatroom" or "blog" (contraction for web log) for this particular shelter. There are communications among "thru-hikers," weather reports, obstacles described to watch out for written by people hiking from the opposite direction, warnings about rats and mice that will try to get your food at

89

the shelter, lost and found items, beautiful scenery not to miss, the spring's location, and anything else that you might want to know.

The logbook in the Laurel Fork shelter located about five miles from Hampton in northeastern Tennessee had a warning for us. The permanent resident of the shelter was a large rat that had been given the name Edgar by previous hikers. From the many notes about Edgar, we learned that he lived in a small hole in the rock shelter wall above the wire-mesh beds. We indeed saw him and even photographed him. Since there were six beds, and six of us, I asked my wife, a farm girl, if she would mind sleeping on the bed just below his perch above our heads. She showed her true friendship by doing that for us. She had experience dealing with rodents because she had cornered a mouse in her house as a young girl, picked it up by its tail, and took it outside and released it.

Appalachian friendship and caring comes from those that you choose to go on trips with, and the generous spirit encountered in others that you meet unexpectedly along the trail is an added blessing.

Backyards, a Life's Journey

Everyone in our country, whether they are wealthy or homeless, has a backyard. The backyard differences are staggering. For example, contrast the differences between those of the Hearst Castle and the Biltmore Estate to the "home under the bridge" and the "park bench" in urban areas. Most of us have backyards that are somewhere between these two extremes. One can also look at our backyards as a timeline for our changing life circumstances. I have had the good fortune of living what would be considered the typical life sequence of backyards filled with both pleasure and pain. Some of us are able to choose our backyards, while others are faced with a backyard that is thrust upon us by circumstances beyond our control.

Not many people are born under a bridge, but Jesus was born 2000 years ago in an equally humble spot with a roof over His head. It was not a very pretty spot, but He was safe with His loving parents. Jesus, Son of God, grew up like a human being, and rejoiced and suffered just as we do.

The first backyard I remember was where my family lived in Kentucky from when I was four to eleven years old. It was a safe, middle class neighborhood in the 1940's. The backyard was much more fun than the cramped house. The yard, like the house, had dimensions that were narrow across the front, but long toward the back. Fortunately, there was a right-of-way for a future street to go between our house and the adjacent neighbor's house so my parents and the neighbor split this space to make both of our yards rather wide. Our backyard and adjacent right-of-way were fenced in with hedges that my father would trim until I was old enough to help. They were beautiful. There was a white, wooden arbor exit from the rear of the hedged yard covered with climbing red roses. My grandmother carefully nurtured these roses as well as a garden of roses having many colors from yellow to dark red. This must have been the start of my love of flowers.

    Inside the hedged backyard we played croquet and swung in a swing. These activities were always lots of fun. Behind the hedge-enclosed backyard there was a grassy area that would eventually become the street and lots for a new development after we moved. My father built two sand horseshoe pits each enclosed with one-inch by six-inch lumber to contain any wildly thrown horseshoes. I played there with my neighborhood boy friends. I will always remember one day when playing horseshoes with my friends, I threw a horseshoe that seemed like a horrible error, but turned out unexpectedly well. I mistakenly pitched the horseshoe high in the air, and it hit an overhanging maple tree limb and slid down the limb tearing off leaves, as it was earthbound, landing perfectly around the stake for a ringer. Our lives have these unmistaken good turns in our backyards, but we usually remember the bad things that happen instead.

    There were woods in our extended backyard that we played in all the time. We played "Cowboys and Indians" and "War" games. It seems like a long time ago, however, it was just after the Second World War had ended. These acts of violence are replaced today with more vivid, but less imaginative video games. The favorite winter activities were building snowmen, snowball fights and sled riding. We built an Olympic-style sled-riding course in our extended back-yard in the woods behind our houses. We cleared out small trees and brush and made it as straight as possible. Some of the big boys in the neighborhood helped us. The course was down a series of steep hills with short flat sections in between. It was like an undulating carpet, and it was so exciting to make it all the way to the bottom without crashing. My life was simple and enjoyable as a child. We were fortunate to own our own sleds, but most games were played using pretend items instead of the real thing. Living in a middle-class household with a spectacular backyard was a joy that I will never forget.

Our extended backyard included a steep mountain cliff we called "Steeplejack". It was Mt. Everest or Denali for a ten-year-old boy. We would take different routes to the mountaintop just as mountaineers do, and we were always proud to stand on top and reflect on our accomplishment of summiting our highest mountain. I remember shortly before moving from this backyard I climbed Steeplejack straight up over an overhanging ledge like you see mountaineers do today using special gear. I never told my mother or dad about that accomplishment because it was dangerous, and I thought I would get in trouble for attempting it.

Everything wasn't just fun and games in the backyard. It also required my doing chores. When I was old enough I was required to cut the grass with a mechanical push lawnmower. If I didn't cut the grass often enough, I had just barely enough strength to push the mower through the tall grass, and that made me mad. Sometimes I would have to cut some sections twice to make it look nice. It made me very mad because I thought my parents made me do things that were too hard for me to do, and other friends didn't have to care for their backyards. Responsibility was something that I was forced to assume, but I guess it was just part of growing up in our family. I also learned eventually that taking responsibility for making the backyard nice looking gave a sense of pride, and made a wonderful place to play.

Our parents decided that the little house was too small for six of us to live in (parents, three children, and grandmother) so we moved to a larger house in an adjoining

Kentucky town that was well known for its good schools. It had a larger backyard plus it adjoined the little used back of the town's park. What a wonderful place to grow up with so many outdoor activities to do. However, we moved in the middle of my seventh grade year away from all my boy friends from the neighborhood and school. Even though it was only about four miles away I had to start over to make new friends, which I found difficult. I played in this extended backyard from the seventh grade until I graduated from high school. My father erected an intricate support system for a basketball goal at the far end of a semicircular patio. Boy friends from school would play here with me. I developed relationships with several boys this way. Living in Kentucky made us avid fans of the sport so we played there a lot. During high school I remember one winter day four of us were playing basketball in the backyard, and it began to snow. We continued to play in the bad weather. The snowy patio was slippery so we would fall occasionally, but we continued to play. My glasses got covered with snow, and got steamed-up, but that didn't stop us from playing either. I paid for this frivolity by getting a very bad cold, and possibly the flu a couple days later.

  We played in the park woods or extended backyard that included a small creek that flowed through the valley below our house. It was fun to play in the creek in the spring and summer, and look for special rocks, tadpoles, and crayfish. Responsibility also followed with this backyard. There was much more grass to cut, and it was much hillier terrain, but now I could use a gasoline-powered lawnmower. I got very good at cutting grass on the sides of the hills in our terraced backyard. This responsibility gave me pride.

  At this age I didn't relate any of nature in the backyard to my relationship with God. I worshiped and studied in church, Sunday school, and youth group, but God seemed separate from my life. I professed that Jesus was God's only Son, and that He died for my sins. With this belief I would have eternal life. I didn't question this belief, but what was it all about? The backyards were just there to enjoy and have fun plus take some responsibility.

The next four years I was an undergraduate student in Kentucky, and backyards were not on my radar screen at all. For the first year in a dormitory, there were other buildings in the backyard, and for the next three years in a fraternity house, the backyard was a paved parking lot. They certainly didn't lead me to thinking about God's presence.

The next year when I was a graduate student in Virginia, I lived in an apartment surrounded by other apartments and fraternity houses with asphalt and some grass. This was my first horrifying experience with a backyard. On Sunday mornings the backyard was covered with glass bottles, broken glass, aluminum cans, empty six-pack cartons, and a lot of paper blowing around. What a filthy mess! I hadn't thought about the beauty of backyards until I observed the antithesis in this backyard. However, with this geographic move to Virginia I lived near the southern Appalachian Mountains for the first time, and experienced the awe of God's earthly beauty. I believe that these contrasting experiences of apparent good and evil may have started me on the journey of feeling God's presence through nature.

My next five years were spent in graduate school in upstate New York. These apartment backyards were rather nondescript except for their color. They were green, covered with grass for eight months of the year, and then white, covered with snow for four months. The snow gradually turned to dark grayish white during March and early April, as the soot from the coal-burning furnaces would fall faster than the new snow. Not a memorable backyard, but there was no time to enjoy it even if it were peaceful.

The next three years I lived in the North Carolina mountains in a townhouse apartment that was more upscale than campus student housing. The backyard wasn't pleasing though, because it was on a busy highway. It was difficult to have a conversation in the backyard because of the eighteen-wheeler trucks flying by the apartment. The problem was noise pollution. Not a good place to contemplate your relationship with God. Since I was finally working, married, and without any children, I had more time. The mountains and valleys within an hour's drive became my extended backyard. It was a real joy, and through mentors I began to feel God's presence in my life through the natural beauty in the extended backyard.

With my wife pregnant with our first child we made a move from a rented apartment to a suburban house in the same city. We lived there for eight years, and it had a wonderful, reflective backyard. There was a small lake next to the house and we spent many hours with our children feeding the fish, canoeing, and walking around this little jewel. Our older daughter named it Blackberry Lake because from our canoe she could pick blackberries that no one else could reach. Our younger daughter referred to the white pines that lined a pathway to the lake in our backyard as "My Forest". She loved to play in her forest, and at four years of age when we eventually moved she wanted to take "My Forest" with her to our new backyard. The joyful feeling for our backyard carried over to me, but now I had an important responsibility. Through God's gift of a backyard he had entrusted me to care for it. For the previous thirteen years while living in apartments I had no clear responsibility for the care of God's Earth. That changed with owning a backyard. We had some wonderful but busy times in this backyard. Viewing Blackberry Lake through a pine-forest-lined path gave me a euphoric feeling. The wonder of God's nature was all around and it gave me a feeling of His presence. It was hard to leave this North Carolina backyard paradise, but job loss required it.

Our current home and backyard in Frankfort, KY, has been our residence for twenty-six years. There is a nice yard with some unique features. It has a wet-weather stream that flows through it which provides an occasional frog, but it is worrisome at times filling in dirt, grass and stones that wash away in a heavy rainstorm. One side of the backyard is lined with viburnum bushes to shield the backyard from the street noises adjoining it. We planted white pines at the back of the yard to provide privacy and serenity for us. Life requires balance, and sometimes it is your children's tough questions that require you to think about it. For example, when our older daughter was about twelve she asked "Why did you plant those white pines in our backyard next to our neighbors? Doesn't it isolate us from them?" Hard question to answer! Her question led us to talk to our neighbors about why we planted the pine trees.

We also have hackberry trees in our backyard. Two of them were positioned perfectly so we could construct a tree house about ten feet above the ground between them. We could climb into the tree house using either a removable ladder or a rope. The tree house was small, but there were many slumber parties and tea parties held in it. Our younger daughter with the help of a neighbor friend devised a human cable car by suspending a steel cable from the front tree of the tree house to another hackberry tree across the yard. They would jump out of the tree house and ride the cable at least halfway across the yard. As the girls grew they became heavier, and we had to first remove the cable because the tree was severely leaning toward the house.

We had that hackberry cut down, and then we removed the tree house, and finally the two hackberries that supported the tree house. In retrospect the kids were just too heavy for the hackberries to sustain themselves with these additional stresses. We were fortunate that none of the trees fell while the kids were playing around or in them. More recently another backyard hackberry fell on our house in an ice storm during the night. Although we had anxiety over the possible damage to the house, it was limited to replacing shingles on the roof and several gutters and downspouts.

Two very large burr oak trees are the highlight of the backyard. We employed an arborist to determine the ages of the trees. He used an instrument that drilled a very tiny, deep hole in the tree trunk, and measured the resultant backpressure on the drill bit as it penetrated the tree to determine the tree's age. The instrument printout showed peaks and valleys that represented the growth rings of the tree. A tree grows fast and the resultant wood is soft during the spring while it grows slowly and produces hard wood the other three seasons. Counting the peaks per inch and knowing the tree radius we estimated their ages to be about two hundred years.

Twenty years ago our daughters loved to sit, bounce, or swing on a low-lying branch of one of the oaks. All their friends loved to do it, but finally the repetitive stress on the limb required its removal. Fifteen years ago the other oak was struck by lightning during a night storm, and scared our younger daughter. We wondered if the tree would survive. Its trunk has healed over the lightning scars and it seems to be growing well. The center branch that was struck by lightening died, and had to be pruned for preserving the tree and the safety of people walking under it.

The burr oak species is one of the few native trees to central Kentucky, and it needs to be preserved. People have asked to collect the very large acorns from our burr oaks to plant for propagating the species while other individuals have used them for ornamental decorations. They are beautiful acorns to see, but if you're pushing a lawnmower under the burr oak trees in the fall, it feels like you are sliding on ball bearings while cutting grass, and poses a risk of falling. The risk is higher when the caps come off the acorn. There is also the risk of injury from an acorn falling on your head. The burr oak acorns provide plenty of food for the large population of squirrels that make their home in our backyard. These burr oaks are the silent sentinels of our years of joy and pain.

We have planted many perennial flowers in our backyard, including columbines, irises, hellebores, coneflowers, and many lily varieties. Also, we transplanted wildflowers such as bloodroot, yellow trillium, and false rue anemone. Their annual rebirth is a symbol of the eternity of God and His presence that I experience in our backyard.

Our older daughter has her own vivid God connection in this backyard. When she was a high school junior she had a serious relationship with Joe, who was a senior. They had much fun playing together in our yard. One of those activities was picking and throwing holly berries at each other. The holly trees were in the front yard. The summer before Joe started college he was killed in a tragic automobile accident. Oh what a horrible waste. Our daughter was devastated. Singing of "Stairway to Heaven," with Christian lyrics during the graveside part of the funeral will always be etched in my soul as will the expression of anguish on my daughter's face. The pain was intense. In the fall of our daughter's senior year she was sitting on the picnic table in the backyard, at least twenty-five yards from the nearest holly tree on the front side of the house. Suddenly a single holly berry fell straight down from the sky and hit her on the leg. She immediately connected to God, and knew that this was a sign to her that Joe was in heaven.

Backyard nature is complex, intricate, and interconnected, and has become a pathway to God for me. For many years I had no understanding of this path, and the spiritual growth resulting from my life's journey of backyards. Retired and sitting in my backyard, my senses are aroused by the invisible wind blowing through the trees with the branches moving like waves in the ocean as the wind passes. It is analogous to the Spirit of God that surrounds us. In our hurried world we miss God's signs such as the flicker pair that nested in a hollow part of one of the hackberries and created beautiful new life. It was sad to see them depart. A squirrel couple replaced the flickers, and raised their offspring in the same backyard home.

My backyards have been symbolic of my spiritual journey thus far. If other backyards beckon in the future, I hope for a place of quiet reflection amid nature.

Let us listen to the solitary bird that warbles its characteristic song saying all is well, and God is with us in joy, pain, and sorrow. Please don't worry about the future; the peaks and valleys of life's journey are our training ground for the spirit life that will follow. Be patient, God has a plan for each of us. We must use all our physical and spiritual senses to discern and implement the plan. There is much noise and disruption surrounding us daily, so we must focus our senses and not miss the song, mystery, and presence of God in His physical and spiritual universe.

Simple or Complex?

On an early fall Sunday afternoon my wife and I visited Cove Spring Park in our city. We go there frequently. It is a park five minutes from the center of town that has several nice hiking trails within the cove.

The park has several springs. A spring results from surface water percolating down through the permeable and porous rock (e.g. limestone) until it reaches an impervious rock barrier (e.g. granite). The water-saturated rock is called an aquifer. When the water reaches the impervious rock, it flows horizontally to an outcrop, where it seeps out of the ground to form a spring. The main springs in Cove Spring Park are thought to come from groundwater that is at least a few miles away.

The spring water from the cove served as the water supply for our city, Frankfort, Kentucky, from the early 1800's until the 1880's. The water is filtered while passing through the aquifer and usually the greater the distance the water travels, the purer it is. In about 1840 a dam was built across the front of the cove to form a reservoir. There are remnants of the dam as well as the thirty-foot high overflow structure still standing. The latter is a magnificent limestone block structure resembling a silo. In the early twentieth century the land was a working farm, but the owners decided to reforest it. Several years ago they sold the land to the city for an urban park. About two hundred yards below the original dam the cove widens into a flat, wetlands area that can be reached by a combination of trails and elevated walkways.

In the cove area of the park a hiking trail called the Holly Loop Trail climbs to the top of the cove. That sunny, early fall afternoon beckoned us to hike this trail. As we hiked, my wife and I saw many blue asters, white asters, and goldenrod in bloom.

High up on the Holly Loop Trail we stopped to rest at a small spring and observed an example of the integration of nature and man-made remnants of the past. A fine stream of spring water was dropping about twelve inches from a moss-covered, rusty pipe, and gently landing in a circular, concrete reservoir about five inches from its edge. The spring water was overflowing the reservoir analogous to a dam's spillway. The small pool was once a watering place for cattle.

Judging from the size of the trees above the small reservoir, we estimated that it was over forty years old. The pool of water was about twelve feet in diameter and twelve to fourteen inches deep. The falling stream of water generated tiny concentric waves the shape of circular arcs that expand to traverse the pool. If one were to imagine this as a miniature ocean, the waves would emulate a tsunami crossing an ocean and hitting the surrounding continents at different times.

A yellow-colored maple leaf gently dropped from a tree overhead landing on the pool without a splash. It was among friends because there were other leaves floating on top of the pool as well as those that could be seen through the clear water on the bottom of the pool. There were this year's leaves as well as rotting leaves from previous years.

Then we saw ever so small random splashes throughout the pool that created their own dainty, concentric circular waves like one observes when throwing a rock into a lake. These waves collided with the waves from the spring water pipe. It was fascinating to observe these physical disturbances on the water surface, but what was causing the little splashes? We ruled out bubbles from the bottom of the pool since moving closer to the pool caused more splashes nearby. There weren't any visible insects on the surface that could have caused this. Then we noticed miniature minnows! I seined a few from the pool and measured their length to be from 9/16 inches to 1-1/4 inches. They were the source of the water surface splashes and associated concentric circular waves. We also observed a frog jump from the wall into the pool with a big splash.

After talking to the city arborist the next day we learned that several Boy Scouts had cleaned out the spring-fed reservoir and placed a wooden bench by it for walkers to rest or meditate. He also told us about the origin of the small fish in the pool. They are called mosquito fish (technically gambusia), and were placed there by the Boy Scouts to protect human visitors from mosquitoes by eating the mosquito larvae. From a Google search I learned that in some states these fish are regulated because they eat other insect larvae and native fish eggs. Of course this is not a problem in this small spring-fed pool. However, it does illustrate that what is a simple solution in one environment can be a complex issue in another.

Observing the pool bottom more closely, besides the leaves, we saw water-soaked sticks, a few large rocks, small limbs sticking out of the water, and some coins. A dragonfly hovered above the pool temporarily.

The details above describe the physical pool that we saw, but superimposed on the actual pool was the image of the surrounding trees with their multicolored leaves and the blue sky. It was a beautiful and serene sight, but also perplexing. One sits down to rest and observe an apparent simple example of nature and man-made remnants, and it turns out to have layers of complexity.

This scene caused us to think about our own lives, and the complexity that exists in them. It also leads to the question, "What is 'real,' and what is 'mirage'?" We can follow what seems to be the pathway that God has been directing us, and then we are startled by failure and suffering. These negative outcomes cause us to question whether we have gotten God's message or whether we are seeing a mirage within our mind and soul. Is this suffering God's way of getting us to grow to spiritual maturity?

We receive God's grace (unmerited favor) because of Jesus' compassion and sacrifice, but the maturation process continues throughout our lives. Characteristics that result from spiritual growth include, "love, joy, peace, patience, kindness, generosity, faithfulness, gentleness, and self-control."[1] These characteristics may seem simple, but they add complexity and depth to our lives just as the spring-fed pool has levels of complexity and interactions that were not immediately apparent. It is difficult to discern the best way to demonstrate love or to be an advocate for peace in the circumstances that we confront in our lives. The process of discovery of the source of the many small concentric waves in the spring-fed reservoir is illustrative of the discovery of the path of spiritual maturity and the "fruit of the Spirit." We need a guide to follow this complex and tortuous path!

Jesus suffered pain and rejection during His earthly life, and made no promise that our earthly lives will be simple or pain-free. The spring-fed pool seemed simple until the reflection of the surroundings added to the scene's complexity. The discernment of God's will is also complex. With constant prayer we can each hope to discover our own path. The journey may appear simple, but the complexity is revealed through contemplation.

[1]Galatians 5:22-23 (NRSV)

Humankind and Nature: Friend and Foe

The stories thus far reflect the beauty, harmony, complexity, and joy that human beings can experience when observing and immersing themselves in nature. Nature provides all the practical benefits of food, clothing, shelter, and even the oxygen we breathe. However, there is another side to these stories that needs to be considered, namely, those times that nature turns against humans. With disasters caused by nature come death and destruction. A natural disaster is any meteorological, geological, weather, or disease caused event that directly or indirectly kills a large number of human beings, other living entities, and destroys property.[1,2] This definition includes only events that are not man-made. Throughout human history, there have been natural disasters caused by earthquakes, tsunamis, floods, hurricanes, tornadoes, and erupting volcanoes. Drought-induced famine and disease are part of the list of natural disasters since they are not man-made.

    The best-known natural disaster story originated in the Middle East, and is recorded in secular and sacred texts. It is described as the "Great Flood", and the hero is named Noah in the Judeo-Christian sacred text version. Noah was directed by God to build a large ark, to capture a male and female of each land-based animal species, and to get them as well as his family into the ark. After Noah accomplished this, rains came, and it rained continuously for forty days and forty nights. In the story the resultant flood covered the entire Earth, but the ark with its species floated safely on the water. All other land-based humans and animals were drowned in the flood. After the rain stopped the water apparently dissipated and eventually exposed dry land for Noah's family and the animals to live on and have a fresh start at life. God promised Noah that a flood of this magnitude would never occur on Earth again.

Sixty-five million years ago there likely was at least one other natural disaster that encompassed the entire planet. That disaster killed over half of the Earth's species including the dinosaurs. The scientific community has been evolving a theory on the dinosaur extinction. The most widely held view is that the Earth collided with a large meteorite. An immense dust cloud formed as a result of the collision enshrouding the Earth in total darkness for a long time. Since the sun's rays were blocked from the Earth's surface, vegetation could not perform photosynthesis. After these plant-eating dinosaurs consumed the existing vegetation, their only food source, they became extinct. To see the other side of the photosynthesis coin one needs only to go to Alaska in the summer when there are eighteen to twenty hours of sunlight per day. It is amazing to observe how fast the vegetation grows!

Natural disasters surely aren't restricted to our planet. Consider the life cycle of the estimated 70 sextillion (70 followed by 21 zeroes) stars in the visible universe, and the living organisms that may exist on planets revolving around these stars. When the star dies from consuming all of its useable hydrogen fuel, it is likely that all the living organisms on the dependent planet will also die. Since our sun is middle age it will not occur on our planet for eons.

On Earth, however, we have witnessed an unusually large number of geological and weather related natural disasters recently. In August 2005 hurricane Katrina became the costliest natural disaster in our country's history. It destroyed infrastructure and property along the Mississippi and Louisiana coasts and in the below-sea-level city of New Orleans. The total death toll was almost 1500. The December 2004 earthquake and ensuing tsunami of South and Southeast Asia killed an estimated 230,000 people, and the October 2005 earthquake in northeast Pakistan killed about 85,000 people. It seems that the developing countries suffer a disproportionate loss of life due to the lack of necessary infrastructure.

Over the last century there have been many more premature deaths as a result of disease and drought-induced famine than from the traditional natural disasters. For example, the 1918-1919 influenza pandemic is estimated to have killed about twenty-five million people worldwide.[1,2] In comparison the death toll from the traditional natural disasters during the whole last century is estimated to be about 3.5 – 5 million.[1,2] The more inclusive definition of natural disasters would increase the estimated death toll from natural disasters for the last century to about 95 million.

The underdeveloped countries of Africa are at very high risk of premature death due to HIV/AIDS and drought-induced famine. For example 1.5 million people in Ethiopia died prematurely due to famine between 1971-73. The death toll from HIV/AIDS in Africa is about eighty percent of the global total of 3.1 million for 2005. As I write this there is a big effort to prevent a possible pandemic of "bird flu." It only rarely passes from bird to human now, but the epidemiologists are concerned about a mutation that would allow the flu to be spread from human to human. The bubonic plague ("The Black Death") of the 14th Century killed 20 million people (33% of the European population), and with our greater mobility in the 21st Century a pandemic could cause the deaths of tens of millions of the world's six billion people.

Returning to the data from the last century, the most reprehensible statistic of all is that humans have killed an estimated 185 million people through wars, oppression, and genocide.[2] The data clearly show that we human beings caused twice the number of premature deaths of our own species than nature did.

When researching the data for natural disasters, I was shocked at the magnitude of evil we do to each other! We in the developed nations have emphasized the mental and material parts of our lives while short changing the spiritual aspects. Compassionate actions come as a result of spirituality in our lives rather than pure self-interest, which causes war. We could find joy in compassionate service to the developing nations to overcome famine, disease, and poverty. Sending the Peace Corps, mission groups, and humanitarian teams could be more effective than sending armies.

Over the millennia of human existence nature has gone from being the enemy that we needed to subdue to being our friend and partner. Although nature does cause death and destruction, we are constrained to rely on it. How wonderful it would be if nature could respond back to us and call the human species a friend and partner. Unfortunately, human culture is continuing to subdue nature as if it were a foe instead of nurturing and sustaining it, as one would do for a friend. To cite a well-known example, it is believed that human activity is causing global warming on Earth that will result in problems for future generations and havoc for the planet. Therefore, the principle of reciprocity currently is out of balance between humankind and nature. To sustain or improve the human condition on this planet, we must make changes now to live more in harmony with nature.

[1] http://www.cbc.ca/news/background/forcesofnature/natural-disasters.html and http://www.answers.com/topic/disaster
[2] Twentieth Century Atlas – Worldwide Statistics of Casualties, Massacres, Disasters, and Atrocities by Matthew White, 2001; http://users.erols.com/mwhite28/20centry.htm

PRAYING

*But when you pray,
go into your room,
close the door and pray to your Father,
who is unseen.
Then your Father,
who sees what is done in secret,
will reward you.*

Jesus

A Prayer for Discernment

Oh God, when I am hiking in the beautiful and serene Appalachian Mountains, it is so much easier to talk to You and express my love because I feel Your presence and hear Your response. There are many who live within these beautiful mountains who don't get to enjoy the Earth's beauty because they are entrapped in poverty. Life is not fair, and I pray to know why, and how to make it become more fair.

Gracious God, the Appalachian example pales by comparison with the millions of peoples who have been unfairly impacted forever by the deaths of over 230 thousand of their relatives, who were killed by the December 26, 2004, Sumatra earthquake and tsunami that followed. I pray for discernment as to why these things happen and what I can do besides praying for the victims and giving monetary donations. The tsunami was an extreme example of a natural disaster, but in the last sixty-five years there are many evil societal examples that show life is not fair. Dear Lord, help me understand the genocide of six million Jews by Nazi Germany in 1943-45, and genocide of over 1.7 million Cambodians between 1975-79 by communist Khmer Rouge through execution, starvation and overwork. There was also the ethnic cleansing of about 250 thousand Muslims in Bosnia by Serbian Orthodox Christians in the early 1990's, and 800 thousand Tutsis that were killed by Hutus in Rwanda, Africa, between April and July 1994. I just don't understand this anger and hatred among people. It's just not fair! Is it because You gave us "free will," and we sin?

Poverty and disease in many third-world countries are also a disgrace. Were these one billion people in extreme poverty [1] (family with income of less than $1/day) destined for this type of life? Jesus said, "The poor you will always have with you, and you can help them anytime you want. But you will not always have me." [2] This must be Your challenge to us to help all the people that are impoverished and ridden with disease.

Religious-based charities, international charities and individuals collectively provide support to the impoverished and diseased as do the United Nations and governments around the world, but it's never enough. We must have our priorities wrong in the "free will" that You have given us. With technological advances, we in the developed countries have more "things" and can be more efficient than ever before, but the resultant faster pace of life gives us less time to contemplate and to pray to You. The complexity of life continues to grow, and can be overwhelming, and what do we gain spiritually? Oh God, the joy and serenity one feels when hiking the beautiful trails in the Appalachian Mountains must be a lesson on how we can live happier, simpler lives. Our relationship with You, our God, and that with our family, friends, and even our enemies can only improve through the desire and discipline to have good communications. That requires us to take time to listen, talk, pray, and take actions of love and compassion.

May the human beings of the Earth say, "Come now, let us reason together" [3] through our love of You, our God, and our earthly neighbors in whatever faith tradition we may practice. Love for You, the Earth, and fellow human beings must negate our overzealous self-interest of being "on the top of the heap," whether it is an individual, a corporation, a religious hierarchy, a city, a province, a nation, or an alliance. I pray to You that I will be patient to listen for Your answer, and that I will be compassionate to others. Amen.

[1] World Bank estimate; [2] Mark 14:7 (NIV); [3] Isaiah 1:18 (NIV)

Pink Lady Slipper Prayer

Oh God, I feel the wonder of majestic glory while lying in nature's pink lady slipper garden. Trusting friends revealed to us the secret abode of these treasures amid the brown carpet of last year's leaves in early May.

After our visit together I had to return alone to commune with You, Oh God, in this marvelous sanctuary. As I lay there I had no concern what others would think because I was alone with You. The squirrels, birds, and a trio of turkeys knew the spot as well. They were content to share it with me at this time. Oh, how this secret pink lady slipper garden restores my soul!

The flower design and construction are superb, Oh God. First to appear are the two basal, ribbed leaves followed by the resolute stem that rises from between the leaves with the bud of a yet unseen solitary flower. As the stem grows taller the green and purple sepals surrounding the bud atop the leafless stem open. Revealed is a magnificent pink flower that resembles a dainty moccasin with red veins where a shoe's laces would be. Oh how unique and resplendent is nature's architecture!

Oh God, how wonderful it is to reflect on the heart-warming experiences You have granted me. I have felt the wonder of Your glory at youth group vespers in the summer of 1956 at Union College. I have felt Your presence with organs in cathedrals resounding Your praise, raising the hair on the back of my neck and sending chills down my spine. I have felt the grandeur of Your universe displayed in the myriad of stars of the Milky Way Galaxy under the clear night dome. I have felt in unison with You!

Oh God, how wonderful it is to reflect on family experiences that showed me Your glory. First gazing on my precious newborn daughters, Beth and Ginger, filled me with awe. Seeing Beth's amazement upon first sight of her younger sister was a blessing. Then much later when Beth became the mother of identical twin daughters, the wonder was repeated. I knew You were there with us.

On a backpacking trip with a friend Your majesty was felt atop Blood Mountain, Georgia. Where were You amid the thunder and lightning of the threatening storm that night? In retrospect You were there as surely as Jesus was at Calvary giving the ultimate sacrifice. You did not abandon Him, nor will You forsake us. As we descended from Blood Mountain on our walk, we discovered a group of pink lady slippers, like the rainbow after the storm, a promise of Your enduring presence. The perfect pink flower is reminiscent of Jesus' perfect life. Oh God, the wonder of how You speak to us! Amen.

BIOGRAPHICAL SKETCH

Richard "Dick" Watkins is a retired development engineering manager from Lexmark International having held similar positions with IBM and AKZO. His career spanned research, development, and engineering in the synthetic fiber and desktop printing industries. The latter included work on inkjet and laser printers and typewriters. He participated in the commercialization of many new products and has ten patents. This is his first collection of memoirs and essays.

    A native of Kentucky, Dick has a BS in Mechanical Engineering from the University of Kentucky, Lexington, KY, and a PhD in Chemical Engineering with emphasis in Polymer Science from Rensselaer Polytechnic Institute, Troy, NY. He lives with his wife Nancy in Frankfort, KY, and they have two grown daughters.